Northwest Flatwater

PADDLING

A Guide to
Lake and Bay Exploration
in Washington and Oregon

by Toby Berry

Facts & Fine Print

Northwest Flatwater Paddling
A Guide to Lake and Bay Exploration in Washington and Oregon.

By Toby Berry

Publisher:	SciScript 15235 SE Bartell Road Boring, OR 97009
Editors:	Lorraine Baker, chief editor Laurie Nock Carol Raizin
Layout/Design:	edk Design 503.644.4459
Cover photographs:	front cover - center photo: Preston Steele - seastarcharters.com back cover - JoEllen Marshall
Photo contributors:	Be' Aspinwall Toby Berry Wendy Duey John Field Ed Kornbrath Roger, Mike & Larry Leverette Craig Lindsay Harold Lyness Herbie Meyer (Northwest Outdoor Center) Laurie Nock

Thanks to Seaward Kayak Company for their support of this project.

Seaward Kayaks
P.O. Box 2026, 610 Oyster Bay Drive
Ladysmith, British Columbia Canada V9G 1B5
1-800-595-9755 Seaward@SeawardKayaks.com

Berry, Toby L.
Northwest Flatwater Paddling, A Guide to Lake and Bay Exploration in Washington and Oregon.
Includes index, maps and photographs

ISBN 0-9706192-0-0
Library of Congress Card Number: 00-192821
Printed in the United States of America

ISBN 0-9706192-0-0

9 780970 619204

Acknowledgements:

To my family and friends
who drove endless roads with me to paddle,
thanks for the fun and
the memories.

To my editors:
Lorraine Baker, Laurie Nock and Carol Raizin,
eternal gratitude for the encouragement
and gentle criticism, and for
making the book right.

To Ed Kornbrath of EDK Design,
thank you for making the book into a book,
and for the seemingly endless map drawing, especially.

To friends and neighbors who picked up the slack at home
while I was out paddling, you make my life work
and I am enormously thankful to you all.

To Bill, Kendra and Wesley —
no work of this size comes without family sacrifice.
Thanks for riding it out with me.

And finally, to the Femmes Afloat,
my kindred spirits because none of you discarded
your adventuresome spirits while raising kids,
thanks for the decade of
adventures together.

I love you all.

Washington & Oregon Trip Regions

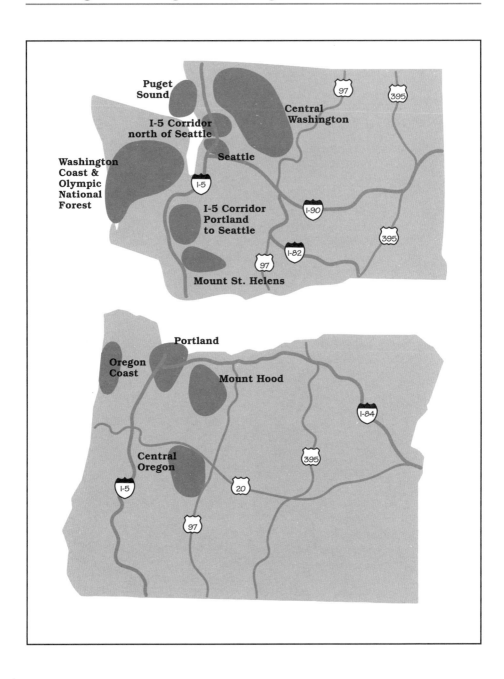

Table of Contents

Part I: Oregon

Part II: Washington

Chapter 10. I-5 Corridor: north of Seattle

Chapter 11. Central Washington

Appendix

Introduction

If you haven't seen anemones while drifting along at low tide, had a seal pop up beside your boat, floated among water lilies or water hyacinths on a mountain lake, or taken a picnic paddle and watched the sun set from a kayak on a calm evening after work, you haven't fully experienced the Northwest.

From Portland to Bellingham, we live and play at the water's edge, but don't often take full advantage of our surroundings.

This book was written to help outdoor enthusiasts explore beyond the shore — quietly.

Whatever your other outdoor interests, you can likely combine them with a kayak or canoe tour. Paddling is for: families, birders, loners, ecologists, environmentalists, fishing enthusiasts, hikers, campers, and swimmers. It is for those who want to picnic, or have a workout away from the confines of the gym. Whatever your related interests, try them from a human-powered boat.

I define flatwater paddling as that which can be accomplished in both directions, as opposed to down-river navigation requiring car shuttle or motor on the water to take you back upstream.

Ratings: My rating system for trips considers water temperature, landing access, trip distance, wind exposure, traffic, and level of marine knowledge required.

- A beginning paddler: One without much navigation experience, virtually no bracing skills, and no rescue practice.
- Intermediate paddler: According to this book, those who have decent endurance to paddle upwind, can get back in a boat confidently with assistance, are acquiring bracing skills and may be ready to go out without a guide in protected salt water environments.
- Expert paddler: Can safely handle all water temperatures because they can roll or brace their way back into a capsized boat, unassisted. Experts can paddle all day comfortably with regard to arm endurance, and they understand and can use tide and current tables. They can instruct and rescue others, when necessary.

Safety Precautions: Though flatwater paddling is relatively safe, any water sport has the obvious inherent risk of drowning or hypothermia. Safety considerations should be foremost. Some basic safety sense includes:

- No matter how good a swimmer, never launch without wearing a personal flotation device (PFD). Like buckling up in a car, this practice is merely basic common sense.
- Know basic capsize recovery, take someone who does, or paddle close enough to shore or in shallow enough water not to need this skill. Almost every shop that rents boats also offers basic rescue courses. Assisted rescues are fun and easy to practice, anyway. My son and I took a basic sea kayaking class together when he was eight years old. The part he liked most was capsizing and getting back in the kayak.

- Don't put a child in a closed cockpit if he/she can't get out of it unassisted. Any child who can not pull a spray skirt off, should not wear one. If you are therefore paddling in an open boat, always follow the shoreline, not making any major crossings. We once paddled a mile across a river on a beautiful day, had lunch and noticed the wind picking up as we finished eating. By the time we were half way back across the river, with my son riding between my husband's legs in an open cockpit, the water was very choppy. As water splashed in on them, filling the cockpit, my husband braced, paddled, and occasionally pumped out the boat until he finally made it to shore. Our son was freezing and frightened, but otherwise okay. We learned a life-saving lesson.
- Kayaks are hard to see from larger boats. Assume that powerboats don't see you and always yield the right of way.
- Paddle directly into any wake. Getting broad-sided by even a small wave often means tip me over and pour me out!
- Have charts with you and know the currents and tides on the ocean. It is easy to get into a tidal rip, ending up on a kayak treadmill fighting the current to the point of exhaustion. Remember that hydro-power is stronger than human power.
- Always have extra clothes along. The sunniest, warmest days can still be cold on the water.
- Always carry water.

Every reputable rental shop rents their boats with flares, floats, rope and pumps included. If they don't give them to you, request them and know how to use them. If you have a cellular phone, take it along, double bagged in ziploc bags if you don't own dry bags.

Maps: Please do not use any maps in this book for navigational purposes. All maps are approximations and are only intended to provide readers with a general layout for each body of water. Maps are not drawn perfectly to scale.

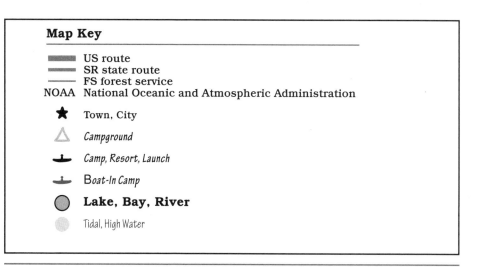

Map Key

▬▬▬ US route
▬▬▬ SR state route
───── FS forest service
NOAA National Oceanic and Atmospheric Administration

★   Town, City

△   *Campground*

⚓   *Camp, Resort, Launch*

⚓   *Boat-In Camp*

⬤   **Lake, Bay, River**

⬤   *Tidal, High Water*

There are other considerations that may not be life threatening but can make the difference between a good and bad experience on the water.

Yikes, I'm not a duck! Know when and where others might be on the water. Bad timing can ruin everything. We once planned a romantic trip, including a stay at an historic bed and breakfast, and a couple days of paddling slow-moving stretches of river near Aberdeen, Washington. Unbeknownst to us, it was opening week of duck hunting season. Though we were easily visible on the water and probably in no danger, hearing gun shots all day long was not my idea of a good time communing with nature. Guns and people in camouflage clothing are not easy to ignore and I had an impossible time enjoying myself on the river.

Even when paddling along a shoreline, there are many spots too steep or rocky to land. Know where landings are along the way so you can plan your rest and pit stops accordingly. Paddling exhausted or in dire need of a bathroom can ruin an otherwise delightful experience.

We headed out on Lake Union for our first time, only to find ourselves buzzed by seaplanes. I've never been so frightened. Later we discovered that we were paddling on the designated sea plane runway. There were no signs on buoys or any warning indicators. To avoid any local hazards, consult the locals or check your maps and charts of the area, even when paddling in seemingly benign areas.

Take extra food and water along, just like you would for any outdoor excursion. You never know when you might end up out longer than you thought. Head winds can slow a trip to a crawl, as can equipment failure, illness or injury. A little forethought is all it takes to avoid hunger and thirst.

Packing list - PFDs and safety equipment including: pump, paddles (including one spare), paddle float, flares, spray skirts and hatch covers should be supplied with all rental boats. You'll need to bring:

- Two pairs shoes and socks (one pair that can get wet, such as an old pair of sneakers, aqua socks, sandals, or neoprene booties). Rubber boots are dangerous. They can fill up with water and sink you, or get caught on deck rigging, or hang you up inside the cockpit.
- Rain gear or better yet wetsuit or drysuit
- Long underwear
- Sweater (wool or pile is best. Cotton, once wet, stays wet and cold)
- Flashlight (just in case)
- Tarp to sit on or under
- Lighter or matches (again, just in case)
- Nylon shorts
- Waterproof bags — Everything can easily be stored in stuff sacks that you've lined with garbage bags to assure waterproofness. Dry bags are great, but not necessary if you aren't ready to invest in accessories.

Family considerations:
If you are taking children along, bring waterproof toys for them to play with en route. Toy boats to pull behind the kayak are perfect, as are fishing poles (equipped with bobbers but no hooks, just for them to watch from the boat).

Also bring sand toys and plan on many landings for kite flying or beach play along the way. Even the most patient children get bored sitting too long if they are mere passengers on the expedition.

Most kids can start solo paddling a small single boat or paddle in front of a double kayak by age 8 or 9. Endurance paddling is another story. Many kids have little.

Finally, don't forget the bird book, binoculars and camera. Any locking baggie works great to keep them dry and handy between your legs in the cockpit.

When you're ready to buy:
If you're ready to buy a kayak or canoe, I strongly suggest going to more than one demo day put on by a nearby rental shop or make an appointment for a private demonstration. Most shops will meet you at a lake and bring several boats for you to try if you're a serious buyer. If you tell them your size and needs, they'll have suggestions and help you narrow down the choices. But ultimately, like buying a pair of shoes, you must try boats on. No one can tell you what is best for you.

Resist the temptation to buy a boat simply because you found a deal on one. You'll likely be sorry you did.

Northwest Outdoor Center on Lake Union in Seattle makes it fun and easy, renting boats by the hour and lining them up dockside.

Basic differences to consider:
Fiberglass boats are longer lasting, lighter and about triple the price of plastic boats. Kevlar is a step up from fiberglass, being lighter, tougher still, and even more expensive.

Don't get intimidated by the jargon. You'll hear talk of primary and secondary stability. All primary stability means is how much the boat rocks back and forth...how tippy does it feel? Secondary stability refers to what it takes to get the boat to actually tip over. The two qualities are not necessarily related. For example, a round-bottomed boat with steep sides may have poor primary stability but excellent secondary stability.

Size-wise, I'd say that a good kayak length for a person is usually about equal to three times the person's height plus a foot or so. It isn't an exact science, but a good place to start. Longer boats are generally faster, but harder to maneuver.

Width-wise is more difficult to gauge. Obviously a skinnier boat is faster, but too narrow a boat can be uncomfortable or too unstable for your ability.

If you are detail oriented, read up on different boats. If you aren't, just go play in them. Once you decide to demo, what should you look for?

- Look for steady tracking (does it veer left and then right as you paddle on the left and the right?).

- See if it stays on course in the wind.

- How maneuverable is it? Test this by seeing how many paddle strokes it takes to turn the boat around? Consider paddling around a marina, being sure you can maneuver the boat in and around other boats.

- How sea worthy is it? Take a bathing suit and see what it takes to flip the boat over.

- Head into a boat wake to test how the boat rides over waves. Some boats give a wetter ride, taking water over the deck every time you encounter the slightest boat wake.

- How comfortable do you feel in the seat?

- Are the pedals easily adjustable?

- How heavy is the boat?

If you're going to splurge on one thing, I'd say, splurge on the paddle. Graphite paddles are expensive ($300 price range) but make fiberglass paddles feel like 2X4's in comparison.

The luxury of a good paddle makes an enormous difference if you're out on the water for hours on end. Try one once and you'll be hooked.

Getting ready to do some paddling.

Part I: Oregon

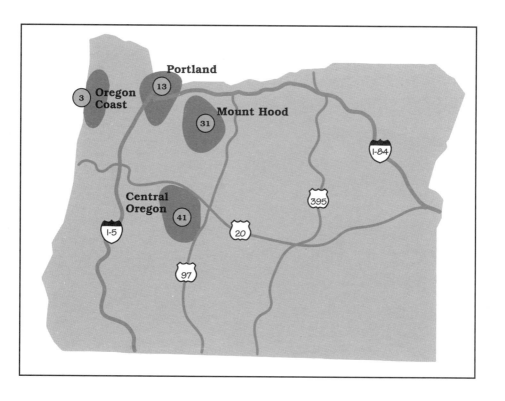

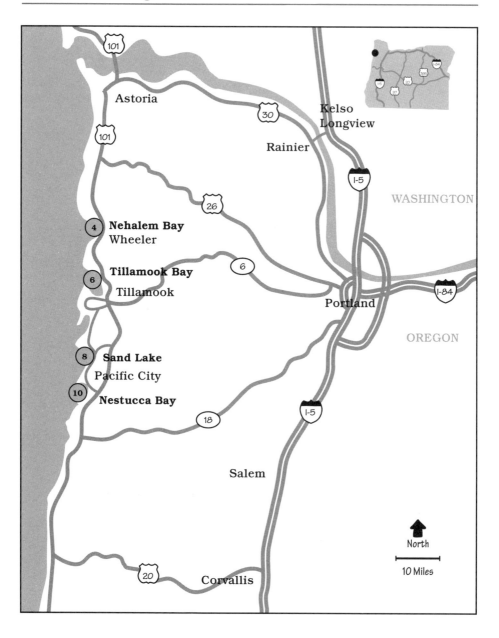

Nehalem Bay

Maps and charts: Tillamook county map, Oregon Coast tour map, USGS Nehalem 15, NOAA chart #18520.

Access: You have several launches to choose from: the public dock in Nehalem, the Tideland boat ramp 2 miles south of Nehalem, or the hotel launch at Wheeler on the Bay Lodge and Marina.

Mileage: Approximately 100 miles from Portland.

Motors: No restrictions.

Directions: Take US 26 east from Portland to SR 53. Head southwest on SR 53 to US 101. If you have your own gear, go north on US 101, and launch at the Tideland boat ramp, just south of the Nehalem River Bridge, or launch at the public dock in Nehalem about a mile north of there, next to Nehalem Dock Restaurant in downtown Nehalem.

If you need to rent kayaks, head south on US 101 to the town of Wheeler and stop in at either Nehalem Bay Kayak Company, on your left, or Wheeler on the Bay Lodge, down the road on your right.

More information: Wheeler on the Bay Lodge and Marina, (800) 469-3204.
Nehalem Bay Kayak Company, (503) 368-6055.
Nehalem Chamber of Commerce, (503) 368-5100.

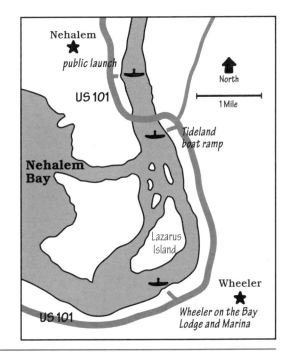

Rating: Beginner to expert

Nehalem Bay is a great day trip for sea kayakers of all levels. You'll almost surely see seal, gull, duck, and heron, but more thrilling is seeing the herd of elk known to swim out to Lazarus Island regularly.

However, like any coastal trip, this one requires planning. Because you can head either upriver or out on the bay, tides are usually not a problem, but do require careful consideration.

If tide is coming in (flooding), go up the North Fork Nehalem River. Be sure to plan enough time to rest, play, and still paddle back at slack water or while the tide is going out (ebbing). Near low tide, there are shallow areas on the river that keep motorboating to a minimum and sometimes cause small boats to ground out.

If the tide is ebbing when you arrive, try launching in Nehalem, perhaps stopping first to eat at the Nehalem Dock Restaurant, which has a deck overlooking the river. You can then paddle down to the mouth of the bay and return at slack water, or on the flood tide.

Don't venture out beyond the protection of the bay unless you are an experienced kayaker. Though the bay may be calm, you can quickly get in over your head on the open ocean. It is difficult to judge open sea conditions from the shelter of the bay, making it easy to paddle into unanticipated swells and white caps.

Also, be sure to head back with enough reserve energy to take on the substantial afternoon headwinds that are likely, especially during the summer. Aside from the danger of paddling upwind on a kayak treadmill, it gets cold on the water. Have windbreakers and sweaters handy, even if you launch in great weather.

One final precaution: It gets choppy when wind and currents oppose one another, even in the protected bay. Afternoons are especially prone to these conditions. Either stay close to shore, where whitecaps are minimal, or take cover by paddling the river instead of the bay when weather or tides dictate.

When everything goes as planned, you can ride the tides in and out and cover some gorgeous territory from the water.

Other attractions: Though Nehalem is tucked in between the larger towns of Cannon Beach and Tillamook, it should not be passed over as a vacation destination. In addition to being a perfect coastal paddling site, Nehalem holds various summer events, including parades, arts festivals, and crab feeds. Call the local chamber of commerce for upcoming activities.

Tillamook Bay

Maps and charts: Oregon state map, Tillamook county map, NOAA chart #18558, Oregon Coast tour map.

Access: Best boat launch is on Bayocean Road, northwest of the town of Tillamook.

Mileage: Approximately 80 miles from Portland.

Motors: Channels are shallow, keeping motors out at low tide.

Directions: Take US 26 to SR 6. Continue on SR 6 beyond the town of Tillamook — the Netarts Highway. Follow the road as it forks to the right (Bayocean Road) heading north, following the bay around toward Cape Meares. The boat ramp is on the right. Fee collected.

More information: Tillamook Chamber of Commerce, (503) 842-7525.

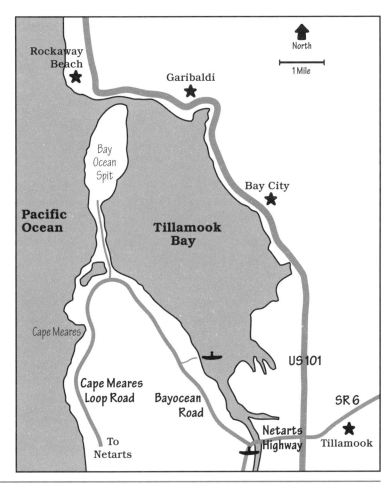

Rating: Expert

Tillamook Bay is tricky for those not completely comfortable navigating the ocean. It looks like one open bay, but the fingers to the south appear and disappear as the tides change. If you have trouble navigating around disappearing landmarks, stay out between the launch and Bay Ocean Spit, which is the only land between you and the open ocean. This route is difficult, however, because there are no landings once you're out on the bay until you get to the spit or the dike. Some of the highest winds I've paddled have been out on Tillamook Bay.

The potential for harsh ocean conditions is high. If all goes well, however, and it stays calm as you head out, you can paddle out to the Bay Ocean Spit, have lunch, and then ride the wind all the way back to the parking lot, fast!

Seals are regulars in the bay, as are several species of waterfowl. Fishing vessels are all over the place at times. Be careful.

Other attractions: Tillamook is the happening spot for ice cream and cheese factory tours, but there are also other annual events. Try the June Dairy Parade or the Tillamook County Fair (early August). If you're ready for a gorgeous coastal hike, check out Cape Lookout.

If you're making a weekend of this paddle, call the Chamber of Commerce to see what else is up.

Sand Lake

Maps and charts: Tillamook county map, Oregon state map.

Access: Launch at Sand Beach in the US Forest Service Recreation Area or at Whalen Island County Park.

Mileage: 100 miles from Portland. Lake mileage: varies greatly with tide.

Motors: 5 mph limit within 200 feet of shore or moorage and 5 mph limit for personal watercraft within 100 feet of non-motorized crafts.

Directions: Take US 26 west from Portland to SR 6. The entrance to SR 6 from US 26 is from the left lane. Take SR 6 to Tillamook, and go left (south) on US 101. From US 101 turn right onto Sand Lake Road to Galloway Road and follow signs to the US Forest Service Sand Lake Recreation Area.

Alternatively, continue on Sand Lake Road to Whalen Island County Park, approximately one mile beyond Galloway Road. Turn right into the park. To get to the gravel launch in the park, take a quick left once you've crossed the bridge.

More information: Tillamook Chamber of Commerce, (503) 842-7525.
Tide tables are available at local hardware stores and listed in the daily newspapers, including the Oregonian.

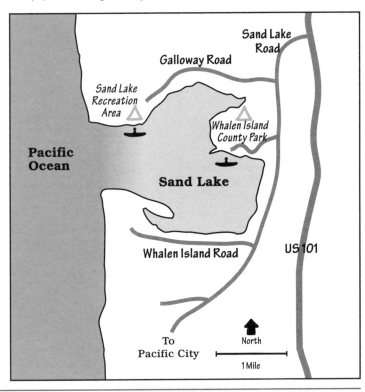

Rating: Intermediate to expert

This trip takes a little planning, because there is no lake at low tide. But, if you leave Portland right at the beginning of a low tide, the lake should be flooded enough when you arrive to paddle for hours. Be mindful to head back to the launch well before the next low, though.

Purchased in August 2000 by Oregon Parks and Recreation, 180-acre Whalen Island is located along the south shore of Sand Lake. Plans are in the works for a state park there. For now, there is a 5-acre county park with a small gravel launch, and camping and picnic areas. This is my preferred parking spot on the lake because it is a shorter walk to the water with boats and because the alternative launch at Sand Lake Recreation Area has all-terrain vehicles available for rent that amass along the dunes there.

Otherwise, both the county park and the recreation area are well-maintained sites to launch, camp, bird watch, or picnic. If you're camping, you can keep your boats at the water near your site in either area, saving extra trips to the boat launch.

Even at low tide, the area is worth the visit, just to sit at the park with binoculars and watch the would-be lake, where birds flock, feed, and squawk. Once the tide rises enough for paddling, but the water level is still too low for motoring, you have a prime paddling environment, with birds still lazing and fishing along the shrinking banks.

Eagle, osprey, otter, seal, deer, cougar, salmon, steelhead, and bear are all reported to live in the area. In my travels there, I've seen all but cougar and bear. Reportedly, five otters reside near Whalen Island Park, though I haven't spotted them there myself.

As always, expect afternoon winds, even in the arms of the lake, which from the map, look sheltered. It is almost always windy at some point during a day trip on Sand Lake and you'll get a good workout. Since there's no getting around some upwind paddling, I rated this intermediate to expert.

Other attractions: Tillamook County is tourist rich, and not without good reason. Plenty to do including visiting the air museum if you're looking for an indoor activity during inclement weather and you've already been to the Tillamook cheese factory. Outdoors, Cape Lookout is well worth the hike.

Nestucca Bay

Maps and charts: Oregon state map, Tillamook county map, Oregon Coast tour map, NOAA chart #18520.

Access: Launch at the boat ramp on the Little Nestucca River.

Mileage: 80 miles from Portland.

Motors: No restrictions, but motorboats can't get up the Little Nestucca River at low tide.

Directions: Take US 26 west from Portland to SR 6. Take SR 6 to Tillamook and go south on US 101 from there. About 4 miles beyond Cloverdale, turn left on Little Nestucca Highway toward Meda and Dolph. Look for Meda Loop Road on your right. Turn there and follow the loop to the launch.

Alternate route: SR 22 west from Salem. In Dolph, the highway forks. SR 22, Three Rivers Highway, heads north at this junction, while Little Nestucca Highway, the one you want, continues west. Less than 10 miles ahead is Meda Loop Road on your left. Follow it around to the small launch site.

More information: Tillamook Chamber of Commerce, (503) 842-7525.

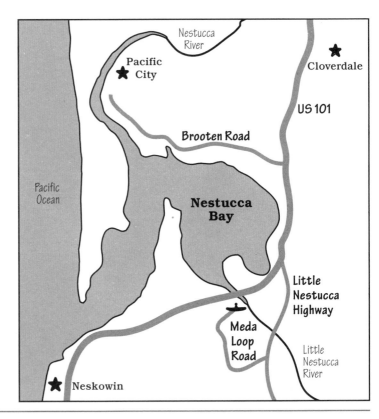

Rating: Intermediate to expert

This paddle is best done when you have a full day to spend and when the current table shows that you can go with the flow, being pushed out toward the ocean in the morning and helped back to the landing in the afternoon.

Whenever we do this trip, we see dozens of seals clamoring around the mouth of the bay. It is advisable to resist temptation, not going out the mouth into the open ocean unless you have open ocean paddling experience and are dressed for the frigid water temperatures. After a visit with the seals near the mouth of the bay you can beach your kayaks for an afternoon of kite flying, paddle ball, frisbee and sand play until the tide turns and floods enough to get back up the Little Nestucca River without grounding out.

Having no restaurants here, you'll probably want to pack a lunch for the trip. We usually pack plenty of sandwiches (which, for our kids, end up with an emphasis on *sand*).

Once the current floods back up river, so can you. Even with an afternoon head wind, as long as you go with the flow, the return paddle is usually manageable.

Other Attractions: The nearest town is Pacific City, up US 101 to Brooten Road. Taking a left on Brooten, you'll land right in the heart of Pacific City. If you cross the bridge in Pacific City you can spend some time at Robert Straub State Park to the left, or Cape Kiwanda State Park to the right. Both are good places to watch the breakers and play in the ocean if it's a warm enough day.

In the town of Tillamook, check out the Tillamook Cheese factory, county museum, and wineries if you haven't ever been.

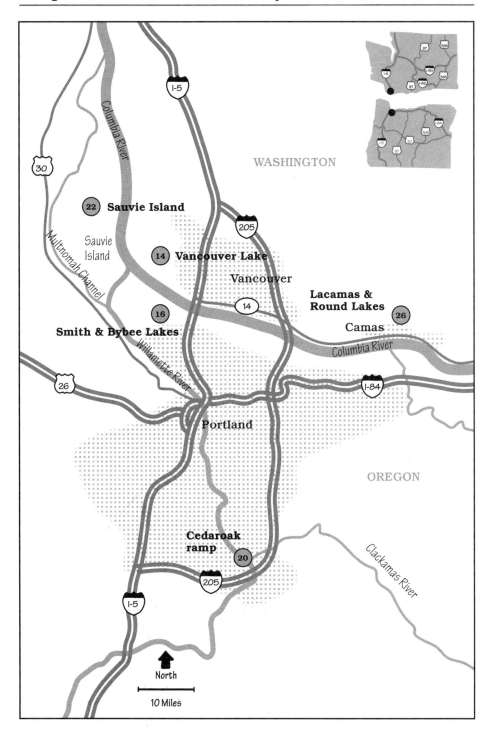

Vancouver Lake

Maps and charts: Vancouver city map.

Access: Launch at the Vancouver Lake County Park or at the ramp less than 1/4 mile before the park entrance. Or, launch on the east side of the lake.

Mileage: Approximately 15 miles from downtown Portland. The paddle is as long or as short as you'd like it to be.

Motors: No motors permitted on the lake, but Lake River, accessed at the north end of the lake, allows motorboating.

Directions: Take I-5 north from Portland into Washington. Take the Fourth Plain Boulevard Exit in Vancouver and head west on Fourth Plain Boulevard. Continue on this road as it curves around to the north and follow it to Vancouver Lake Park. Park entrance fees are collected during peak hours.

If you want to launch on the east side of the lake, take I-5 north to 39th Street in Vancouver and head west from there. Turn left where it ends at Fruit Valley Road and right in front of Fruit Valley Park on La Frambois Road. Follow the road until it ends at a quiet launch on the lake. There is a nominal fee to park and launch here.

To do a car shuttle to the town of Ridgefield, continue north on I-5 to the Ridgefield exit. Turn left on SR 501. Turn right on South Third Street and left on Mill Street, until you reach the launch site. There is a small fee to park here, also.

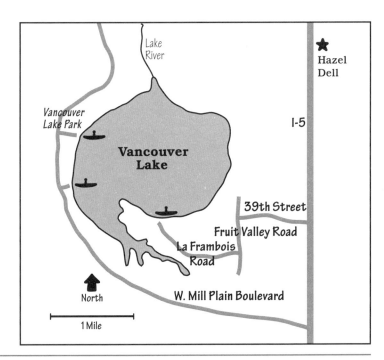

Rating: Beginner

Vancouver Lake is usually calm and the water is shallow— averaging 8 to 12 feet. It's the perfect spot for a family paddle or to practice rescue skills. Because of the shallow depth, the lake warms up enough for swimming, too.

Not only is the lake close and convenient for urban escapees, but the park is a nice place to visit with or without boats. There are picnic tables, paddleboat and windsurfing rentals, and there is also a sandy area for beach play.

As for the paddling itself, the biggest threat is probably the carp that sometimes smack the sides of the boat when they're touched by a paddle. Obviously no real danger, but it sure is alarming to be paddling along quietly and have one slap you upside the boat.

Paddling north from the park, you'll come to Lake River. The river is approximately 2 miles from the park. Paddling up the river provides some shelter from the wind, should you need it. Lake River eventually connects to the Columbia River around Sauvie Island, almost 20 miles to the north. The river is tidal, so if you want to paddle that far, plan to go with the flow, if possible.

Approximately 16 miles north of Vancouver Lake on Lake River is the town of Ridgefield, which also has a boat ramp. This makes for a nice car shuttle paddle, but the lake itself is nearly 3,000 acres, which can keep most paddlers entertained without ever going up river.

Once, we lunched and then launched at Vancouver Lake Park with an eagle watching us. The majestic bird was perched about 25 yards away, eyeing us as much as we were eyeing him.

Aside from eagle, osprey, and great blue heron, this lake is also a fishing paradise, populated with catfish and bass to name just a couple. Vancouver Lake is a fun place to try fishing from a kayak.

To top off the paddling ambiance, Mount St. Helens and Mount Hood are both visible from the middle of the lake on clear days.

Other attractions: After a day's paddle, try Who Song and Larry's Mexican Restaurant — a lively spot to eat along the north shore of the Columbia River in Vancouver.

Smith & Bybee Lakes

Maps and charts: Portland city map.

Access: Launch at Smith and Bybee Lakes parking lot on Marine Drive.

Mileage: Urban paddle in Northwest Portland.

Motors: Electric trolling motors only.

Directions: Take I-5 north from Portland to the N. Marine Drive exit. Go northwest on Marine Drive for approximately 3 miles to the clearly marked parking lot.

More information: There are plans to build a new parking lot and access directly into the lake. Call Metro for more information about parking changes.
Metro Regional Parks and Greenspaces, (503) 797-1850.
Metro wildlife manager, (503) 797-1515.
Friends of Smith and Bybee Lakes - Frank Opila (503) 283-1145.

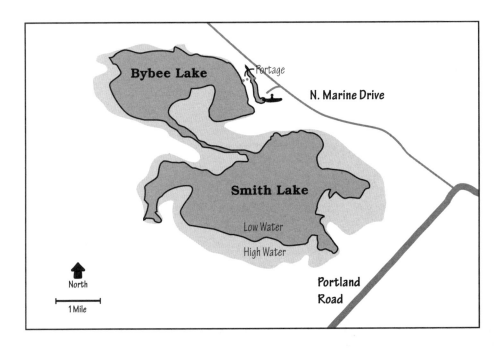

Rating: Beginner to intermediate

Smith and Bybee Lakes are an urban paddler's gold mine. It is embarrassing to admit that I'd lived in the Portland area for 15 years before ever checking it out. Some guide books describe this paddle as having poor access and requiring portages, turning me off to the area. Well, that has changed some. The most recently built parking lot is clearly marked and easy to find. And the portage into Bybee Lake, from the slough you originally launch in, is only about a 150-foot carry. Some folks strap wheels on the bottoms of their boats to assist in portaging. These wheels are available for sale or rent in most boating shops.

The launch from the parking lot into the slough is so narrow that it is a one-at-a-time put-in, but it isn't difficult to help each paddler in, leaving the strongest paddler to launch last.

The unnamed slough is home to one of the largest populations of Western painted turtles in the country. They bask on logs all around. If you don't want to portage into the lake, you can spend plenty of time just in the half-mile long slough, watching birds, ducks, and turtles, among other wildlife.

Only a quarter mile or so up what I call Turtle Slough, on your left, is the portage into Bybee Lake. There are power lines across the water here, which is your portage landmark. Once you've portaged over to Bybee Lake, there is a flat and wide spot to lunch or walk around before launching again. Many of the other potential landings are marshy and uninviting, so take advantage of this area if you need to.

Smith & Bybee Lakes

If you paddle directly across the lake and follow the shoreline along, you'll find many channels that lead into the larger Smith Lake. Both lakes and the channels connecting them are rich with life.

Expect to see beaver, or at least their dams and lodges, which are prevalent throughout the area. Also, no doubt, you'll see heron and osprey. Over 100 species of birds visit the area, including peregrine falcon. The most spectacular I've seen were four American white pelicans that flew over us in a line with their nine-foot wing span. Almost touching, as if holding hands as they flew, the birds landed right in front of us on Smith Lake. I talked about it for weeks. Watch for bald eagle on both lakes, especially in winter. Otter and deer are often spotted on land or in the water all over the wetland. The lake swells with large-mouth bass.

Unlike on the Willamette or the Columbia rivers, on this urban paddle, you'll feel miles away from it all. The area is quiet, since no gas-powered motors are allowed, and you are treated to a distant view of Mount Hood on a clear day.

Smith and Bybee Lakes encompass over 2,000 acres, so there is plenty of paddling to do here. But, there is also a loop hiking trail around the lakes for those ready to get off the water and stretch their legs.

Incidentally, there is an outhouse just a short distance up this trail from the parking lot.

If you fall in love with the area, consider joining Friends of Smith and Bybee Lakes. They serve as watchdogs, helping prevent development near the lake. They organize paddle trips, bird watching walks, work parties to help maintain the area, and help schedule school field trips into the wetland.

Other attractions: There is plenty of hiking to do here, and also an annual Smith and Bybee Lakes Day, with educational booths and activities for kids along the trail around the lake. You aren't far from the Jantzen Beach Mall, REI, and Alder Creek Kayak and Canoe, for eating and shopping opportunities. A favorite eating spot for us is the Island Cafe, accessed from the Alder Creek parking lot. The eatery is built on the dock looking out on the Columbia River from Tomahawk Island. Nothing fancy, just good food right on the water.

Portage from the slough to Bybee Lake.

Cedaroak ramp

Maps and charts: Portland city map, NOAA chart #18528.

Access: Cedaroak boat ramp in West Linn.

Mileage: Round trip approximately 5 miles to Oregon City Locks and back.

Motors: Shallow areas around the launch allow some isolation from motors.

Directions: From Portland take SR 43 through Lake Oswego to the town of West Linn. Turn left on Cedaroak Drive, north of Mary Young Park. The road loops you around Cedaroak School to the bank of the Willamette River.

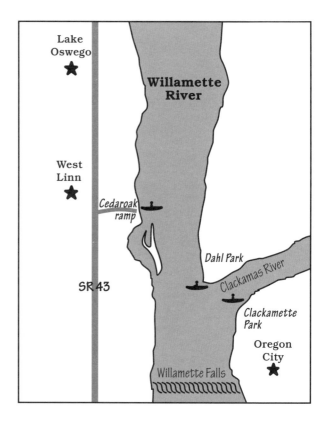

Rating: Beginner to expert

Cedaroak is a popular small-boat launch. You may have to weave around fishermen and motorboaters midday in midsummer. But, because of the easy access, it is possible to avoid some of the motorist hazards by heading out for a sunset paddle as boat traffic subsides. Motor traffic also drops off drastically in less-than-perfect weather, so it is also a prime-pick paddle on cloudy days.

Heading upriver first is always a good idea, because it makes the return trip less difficult. From the Cedaroak ramp, paddle up the Willamette River and cross to the east bank, to Clackamette Park. The park is a nice, easy landing spot for picnicking and even flat enough for frisbees and kites. Beyond the park, paddle under the I-205 bridge to Oregon City, until you reach the locks at Willamette Falls. Don't paddle too close.

If you go east at the park, paddling up the Clackamas River instead of continuing up the Willamette, you have a fun upstream paddle for a short distance until the water starts to riffle. This is not a path for beginners, but a great place for more experienced paddlers to practice their rolling and bracing skills.

For a slower pace and more serene ambiance, along the west bank of the Willamette River, just upstream from the Cedaroak launch, there is an enclave of homes and a section of quiet, still water, too shallow for motorized crafts. It was here, at dusk, that a friend and I saw a green-backed heron. The bird landed on the bank in front of us, as if this were her permanent home — watch for her.

Great blue heron, beaver, and common mergansers all frequent the area. Vultures abound too, usually scavenging on washed up fish parts left by fishermen.

Other attractions: West Linn and Lake Oswego have plenty of restaurants to choose from if you're hungry after your river excursion. As a memorable and relaxing way to unwind, try paddling up to a riverside restaurant for dinner some evening.

Sauvie Island

Maps and charts: NOAA chart #18524, USGS Sauvie Island and St. Helen maps, Portland city map, Oregon state map, Sauvie Island map, available at the Sauvie Island Wildlife Area office at 18330 NW Sauvie Island Road.

Access: Numerous launches, but this chapter discusses the Columbia River to Bachelor Island at the end of Reeder Road, and the Gilbert River. Buy a Sauvie Island parking permit at the Cracker Barrel Grocery on NW Sauvie Island Road, GI Joes, or Walmart. It is required everywhere on the island.

Mileage: Approximately 10 miles north of Portland.

Motors: Much of the Gilbert River is shallow and impassable by motorboat.

Directions: Take US 30 northwest from Portland toward the town of St. Helens. Turn right over the Sauvie Island Bridge, then head left (north) on NW Sauvie Island Road to Reeder Road. Go right on Reeder Road, then follow it to the left, eventually heading north along the Columbia River. Near the end of the road turn left directing you to the boat launch (Gilbert River) or take Reeder Road to its end to put in on the Columbia River.

More information: Alder Creek Kayak and Canoe, (503) 285-0464.
Ebb and Flow Paddlesports, (503) 245-1756.
Sauvie Island Wildlife area office, (503) 621-3488.
National weather service (flow phone), (503) 261-9246.

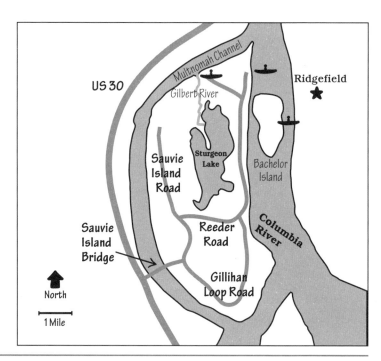

Rating: Beginner to expert

Sauvie Island has some of the best paddling in the state with regard to variety, wildlife viewing and access. But, rules change regularly out there and detailed, accurate information is hard to come by, according to one Ebb and Flow Paddlesports employee. Some current rules you need to know are: Sauvie Island interior is closed to paddlers from Oct.1 - April 15th. If you are out there at that time, you can only paddle the Multnomah Channel, the Willamette River, or the Columbia River. But, don't miss the time right before or after the closed season, as those are the best times to see migratory birds such as sandhill cranes and tundra swans.

You can often see bald eagle, especially directly across from the Sauvie Island Kennel on Reeder Road.

Fires are not allowed on the island, even on the beach along the Columbia River. Enjoy a sunset picnic after paddling, but keep any pyro tendencies in check.

Another important warning is that Sturgeon Lake water levels fluctuate up to 4 feet per day with tides. Paddlers have been stuck in mud out there and had to be airlifted out. I avoid Sturgeon Lake, as there are other great paddling opportunities from the island. Still, if you want to paddle there, check tide tables and avoid Sturgeon Lake during low tide on the Columbia.

Finally, the Columbia River side of the island is exposed and winds come up fast. Be sure to reserve enough energy for a return trip with a headwind. Avoid crossing the Columbia at all during high winds unless you have some bracing experience, and be careful of the large ships along the river.

Don't let these precautions discourage you from paddling Sauvie Island altogether. The Gilbert River is a quiet paddle, even on busy summer days. This is a great place for beginners, as it is easily navigable, well protected from high winds, and, except for small trolling boats, motorboats generally avoid the area. You can land anywhere that isn't too steep. Take a tarp to sit on, as there are some marshy areas along the banks. For a change of pace, try an evening paddle here during our long summer days.

If you go to the end of Reeder Road to launch on the Columbia, don't be surprised to see nude folks wandering the shoreline. This is a clothing optional area.

As far as the paddling goes, if you aren't an experienced paddler yourself, or you aren't at least accompanied by one, stay close to shore. Remember to turn your boat into any large wakes. This is the only place I've capsized my boat, unplanned. I turned around to see the size of the wake a recently passing ship had kicked up and found I'd reacted too late. Broad-sided by a wave, I braced and was enjoying riding the wake when a wave came back at me from shore and dumped me. Fortunately, the water was warm and shallow and I was able to retrieve all my belongings before they sank.

If you are ready for a bigger challenge (sometimes this paddle is easy, but don't count on it) cross over to the east side of the Columbia River and paddle around Bachelor Island. The east side of Bachelor Island is rich with bird life and sheltered from the winds along the exposed Columbia. The trip circumnavigating Bachelor Island and returning to the west bank of the Columbia is approximately 10 miles. This is a great training paddle as a dash after work in summer for paddling marathoners or others paddling for fitness.

Watch for eagle, osprey, heron, geese, duck, river otter, black-tail deer and the aforementioned migratory birds anywhere on Sauvie Island.

Other attractions: From the pumpkin patch to the nursery, Sauvie Island is a wonderful place to take visiting friends and relatives. Birdwatching and bike riding are also common activities on the island. Alder Creek Kayak and Canoe offers regular group paddling trips on Sauvie Island if you aren't ready to venture out there on your own.

A glassy surface, no wind and sunshine.

Lacamas & Round Lakes

Maps and charts: Washington state map, Camas city map.

Access: Pullouts along the east side of Lacamas Lake, a public launch half way up the east side of the lake (Access Stewardship Decal required for parking) and access at Lacamas Park, with Lacamas Lake on one side of the road and Round Lake on the other.

Mileage: Approximately 30 miles from Portland. Lacamas Lake: Approximately 3 miles long. Round Lake: Approximately 2 mile perimeter (40 acres of water).

Motors: No combustible motors on Round Lake. Lacamas Lake has motorboats, but large no-wake zones and shallow areas at the north and south ends of the lake.

Directions: Take I-5 or I-205 to SR 14 East in Washington, toward Camas. Take the first Camas exit, Exit #12, onto NE Sixth Avenue. Go left onto Dallas Road then right on NE 15th Avenue, then left again on NE Everett Street. Follow Everett a short distance to Lacamas Lake on the left and Round Lake on the right at Lacamas Park. At the south end of the Lake, you can park and put in at the park on Round Lake and paddle under the road bridge into Lacamas Lake if water levels are low enough to get under the pipes under the bridge, or you can just paddle Round Lake. If you continue past the park veering right onto Leadbetter at the fork, there are a couple launch spots as you drive up the east side of Lacamas Lake.

More information: Camas Chamber of Commerce, (360) 834-2472.

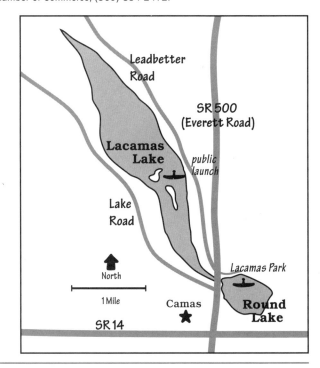

Rating: Beginner to intermediate

Round and Lacamas Lakes are great for afternoon getaways, or part-day trips. Not that you can't find enough water to keep you busy all day, it's just that the lakes are so close to Portland that it is possible to get away midday and still get in a good paddle, especially on summer evenings when days are long.

There is no camping in the area, which also makes this a good short-trip paddle. I like parking at the Lacamas County Park, at the south end of the lake if the access to Lacamas Lake from Round Lake is passable. That way, if things get too busy, motor-wise on Lacamas Lake, it is easy to seek refuge on the smaller, no-combustible-motors-allowed Round Lake. If you do opt to launch here at the park, you'll have a much shorter walk to the water if you enter the lake at the second park entry, by turning right onto Leonard Road from Leadbetter Road, then right into the launch area across from the overflow parking lot.

I also recommend launching at a pullout along Leadbetter Road about two thirds of the way up the east end of the lake, where Leadbetter Road turns to 232nd. The short trail to the water from the pullout is easy to walk with a kayak or canoe, and gives the quickest access to quiet and shallow Lacamas Creek at the north end of the lake.

Also on Leadbetter Road, but only about half way up the lake, is a large parking area and public launch. Access Stewardship Decal permits are required at this parking lot, and are available wherever fishing/hunting licenses are sold.

Lacamas & Round Lakes

For paddlers interested in birding, I am told the spring and fall on these lakes is spectacular. Even in midsummer we saw wood ducks, plenty of heron, osprey, mallard, kingfisher and Canadian geese. As for other wildlife, we also came across nutrias, which look like beaver, but with rat-like, round tails.

If you choose to paddle these lakes on a summer weekend, you may want to stay at the south end of the lake in the no-wake area, or on Round Lake which is skier free. The best spot to be on a busy weekend, though, is on the north end of the lake and up Lacamas Creek, which leads to miles of shallow, marshy waters. Paddling through pond lilies and following the lake as it twists and winds, like switchbacks up a mountain, makes for a most relaxing trip, free from most motor-boat traffic.

If you are in the main body of Lacamas Lake on a busy day, avoid the lake's center strip, as you'll find it laden with waterskiers. Beware of seaplanes, as well.

The west side of Lacamas is all private land, with no launching or landings available on Lake Road as it parallels Lacamas Lake unless you are a Moose Lodge member or a Lacamas Shores resident.

Other attractions: For a quick cool-down, or if you're in need of a little excitement to jazz up your lazy afternoon, try a ride on the rope swing, about a third of the way up the lake on the south end of a small island. Hanging from a large tree, this rope accelerates your refreshing plunge into the lake. Off the water, downtown Camas comes alive on the fourth weekend of July during Camas Days, where you can enjoy parades, jazz music, and wine and microbrew tasting.

Chapter 3: Mount Hood

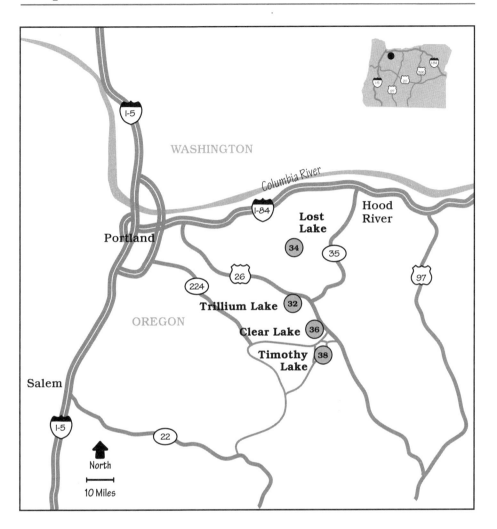

Trillium Lake

Maps and charts: US Forest Service Mount Hood National Forest map.

Access: Boat ramps at day use area and campground, and several other parking spots that you can walk your boat down to the water from.

Mileage: Approximately 60 miles from Portland. Paddling mileage: 2 miles round trip.

Motors: No motorboats allowed.

Directions: Drive US 26 east from Portland up Mount Hood. Turn off at the Trillium Lake turnoff and drive 2 miles to the lake.

More information: Forest Service Mount Hood Information Center, (888) 622-4822. Campground reservations (National Recreation Reservation Service), (877) 444-6777.

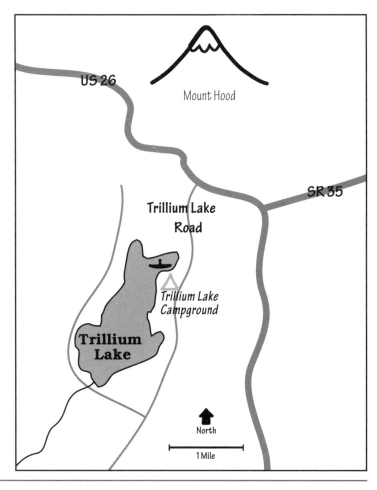

Rating: Beginner

Trillium Lake is the perfect choice for paddling destinations if you want an alpine experience close to Portland.

The only drawbacks are that the lake is quite small, the perimeter being only 2 miles, and the lake is frozen over in winter, open for boating and camping usually from Memorial Day through Labor Day only.

Once you get to the lake, there are boat ramps for launch at the day use area and the campground. Parking at the day use area instead of the campground will save you some money, though.

As is true in all the Northwest alpine lakes, afternoon winds pick up almost every summer day, but since it's such a small lake, you shouldn't have any trouble getting around it, even on a windy afternoon.

The lake is popular for trout fishing, with dozens of inflatable rafts on the water on hot summer days. The winds are significant for those vessels. One man in the parking lot admired our kayaks enviously, telling us what a difficult time he and his friend had rowing their raft across the lake.

The trail around the lake is gorgeous and so well maintained with boardwalks and blacktop that it is an easy walk, even with toddlers, should you want to take the family and hike as well as paddle.

As far as what you'll likely see on this trip, the Mount Hood views are spectacular from land and water on clear days.

Also, though there are trilliums around the lake, expect to see several other alpine wildflowers in bloom. Floating on the lake, yellow pond lilies abound and even obstruct paddling in places as they thicken throughout the summer.

People swim in the lake, though it was still a bit chilly for me in late June.

There is a fee to park, even in the day use area.

For overnighters, campground reservations are recommended.

Other attractions: Timberline Lodge is always worth a visit. The food and beverages there are excellent, though costly. Other hikes and paddles are worth checking out, too. See Timothy and Clear Lake sections.

Lost Lake

Maps and charts: US Forest Service Mount Hood National Forest map, Oregon state map.

Access: Launch at the small-boat launch on the lake, turning left where the road forks once you've reached the lake. If renting a boat, turn right and arrange for the boat rental at the general store. Entrance fee required no matter where you park.

Mileage: 85 miles from Portland. Lake mileage: Approximately 3.5 mile perimeter.

Motors: No motors allowed.

Directions: Take I-84 east from Portland. Take Exit #62, the first Hood River exit. Go left toward the Hood River main drag. Turn right on 13th Street. Follow it through Hood River, southwest to Odell and Dee. Veer right toward Odell/Parkdale, then left onto Tucker Road. Follow signs to Lost Lake. You wind through Hood River, past the fire station and around the cemetery. They don't call it Lost Lake for nothing.

Alternately, take Exit #64, follow US 35 to Hill Drive. Turn right on Hill, left on Lindgren where Hill ends, right on Ehrck Road, which turns into Summit Drive. Follow Summit Drive to Dee and follow signs to Lost Lake from there.

Final alternative: US 26 toward Mount Hood. Turn left onto Lolo Pass Road in Zig Zag and follow signs from there.

More information: Lost Lake Resort, (541) 386-6366.
US Forest Service Mount Hood Information Center, (888) 622-4822.
Campground reservations, first come, first served.
Columbia Gorge Hotel, (541) 386-5566.
Mount Hood Railroad, (800) 872-4661.

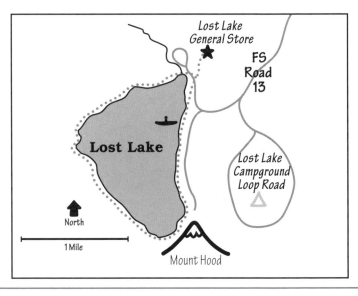

Rating: Beginner

This is a late afternoon getaway as opposed to a full day paddle, because the lake is fairly small. You could combine this paddling adventure with other interesting things to do in the area and spend more than a day on the north side of Mount Hood, though.

One afternoon, I left my house at 3:00 p.m, and drove up to take my puppy on his maiden kayaking voyage. I paddled the lake, saw a bald eagle, an osprey, and a merganser with 5 ducklings, and got home in time to sit with the family and sip a margarita on the deck before bed. It really is a quick, easy getaway from the city.

The view of 11,000+ foot Mount Hood is fantastic. We usually gaze at the mountain looking at its west or south face, rarely seeing the north side, so this view is a special treat. The campground and hiking trails are nice, but often popular on weekends. A general store, rustic cabins, paddleboats, rowboats, and canoes are available at Lost Lake Resort.

Aside from the mountain view, expect to see rhododendron and lupine in full bloom from late June through mid-July. The fishing is good, with several species of trout and kokanee salmon in the lake. Because of the elevation (3,100+ feet), the area is closed in winter. Typically the season runs from May to October.

Finally, you can't go to Lost Lake without stopping at the Old Trunk bookstore and produce farm, on your right as you head up Lost Lake Road. The character and history of the place almost equals that of the books within.

Other attractions: The Mount Hood Railroad offers an assortment of rail adventures nearby. The Columbia River Gorge Hotel multi-course brunch (I lost count) in Hood River is elaborate. We call our trips there the Gorge and gorge, as we always leave there with a need to work off our food.

Clear Lake

Maps and charts: Oregon state map, US Forest Service Mount Hood National Forest map.

Access: Boat ramp at campground.

Mileage: Approximately 70 miles from Portland. Paddling mileage: 8-10 miles around the lake.

Motors: 10 mph maximum speed on the entire lake.

Directions: Take US 26 east from Portland up Mount Hood. Approximately 10 miles beyond the US 35 turnoff, still on US 26, is the turnoff into Clear Lake Campground.

More information: US Forest Service Mount Hood Information Center, (888) 622-4822. Campground reservations, National Recreation Reservation Service, (877) 444-6777.

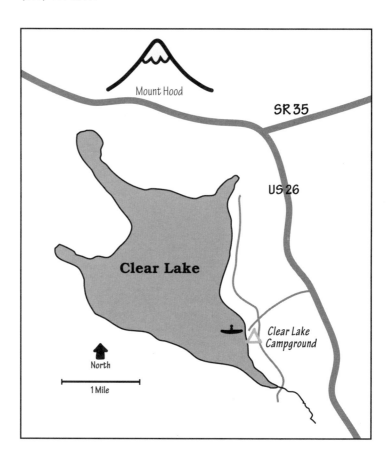

Rating: Intermediate, because of wind conditions

Clear Lake is approximately 2 miles beyond Frog Lake (which is pretty, but in my opinion too small to unleash kayaks into).

Clear Lake, however, is much larger than Frog Lake and has nice arms to paddle up. The only problem with Clear Lake is that it is relatively exposed. The winds often don't die down until late in the evening, and were still howling at 7:00 p.m. when we were there in late June. Still, the views are pretty and the lake is large enough to make for a good day's paddle.

Many locals enjoy fishing for trout, and this is definitely a possibility from a kayak or canoe. The low speed limit keeps water skiers and jet skiers out. Primarily, you'll be sharing the lake with small trolling boats.

It is possible to see deer and other mountain wildlife around the lake. Osprey were prevalent, but surprisingly few ducks were on the water when we were there.

There is a fee to camp at the lake and, if you leave your car there, you may be required to pay, even if you're not planning to camp.

Other attractions: There are several other things to do nearby, including hiking at Frog Lakes Butte, just up the road, and dining at Timberline Lodge – always worth a stop for good, though expensive, food and drink. If you want to do a loop drive after paddling, you can continue down Highway 26 less than 10 miles to Timothy Lake and follow directions from the Timothy Lake trip description back to Portland through Estacada. The drive along the Clackamas River is pretty, you can stop and picnic at Promontory Park, and this route is no longer than returning the way you came on Highway 26.

Timothy Lake

Maps and charts: US Forest Service Mount Hood National Forest map.

Access: Oak Fork Campground, Gone Creek Campground, Hoodview Campground, Pine Point Campground. All have easy access to the water, but there is a campground fee whether you stay overnight or not. The parking area at Meditation Point trailhead at the northwest side of the lake is recommended as the paddling in this area is more protected from the weather.

Mileage: Approximately 75 miles from Portland. Lake mileage: 17-mile perimeter.

Motors: 10 mph speed limit.

Directions: Drive I-205 south from Portland to SR 224, east toward Estacada/Mount Hood. Stay on SR 224 following the Clackamas River to Forest Service Road #42 toward Breitenbush and Detroit Lake. Turn left on Forest Service Road #57 toward Timothy Lake. This intersection had no visible road number but was marked "Timothy Lake."

More information: Forest Service Mount Hood Information Center, (888) 622-4822.
National Recreation Reservation Service (camping reservations),
(877) 444-6777.

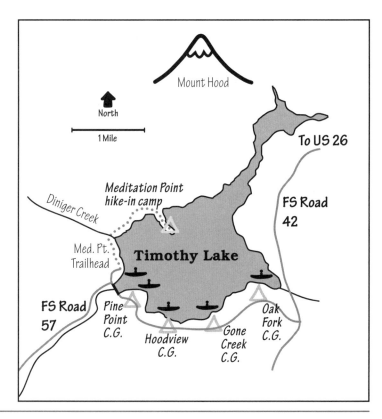

Rating: Beginner to intermediate

Timothy Lake is one of the closest alpine lake paddles if you live in southeast Portland or the Salem area. The largest of the Mount Hood lakes listed in this book, Timothy Lake, also has better wind protection. There is plenty of lake to paddle, hike, camp, and fish, and the view from Hoodview Campground is post-card-perfect. The mountain flora is rich with Indian paintbrush and other high mountain wildflower classics.

Paddling up to Diniger Creek and northeasterly is worth the venture for the quiet at that end of the lake. Because of the speed limit restrictions, there isn't terrible motor noise, but the campgrounds get busy in summer.

Still, a moonlight paddle to the north side of the lake is quiet enough to make you forget that you're only an hour from downtown Portland.

Chapter 4: Central Oregon

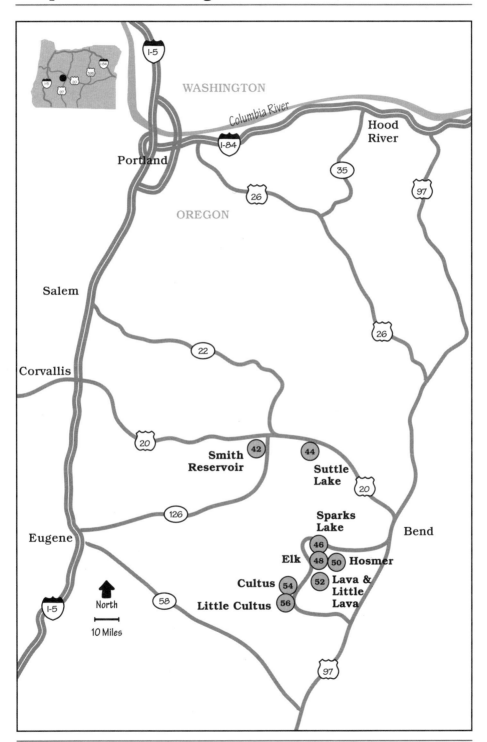

Smith Reservoir

Maps and charts: US Forest Service Willamette National Forest map, Oregon state map.

Access: There is one launch on the south end of the reservoir.

Mileage: 40 miles west of Sisters, approximately 150 miles from Portland. Lake mileage: 2 miles long.

Motors: 10 mph speed limit.

Directions: Take I-5 south from Portland to Albany. Head east on US 20 from Albany along the Santiam Highway. Go right (south) on SR 126 until you get to Forest Service Road #730 leading to Smith Reservoir and Trail Bridge Reservoir. Turn right onto Forest Service Road #730, go beyond Trail Bridge Reservoir and follow the road up to Smith Reservoir.

More information: Sisters Chamber of Commerce, (541) 549-0251.
McKenzie River Ranger District, (541) 822-3381.

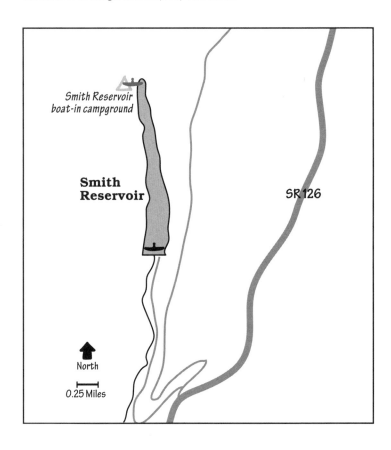

Rating: Beginner to intermediate

The best thing about this tour is the small campground at the top of the reservoir. A two-mile paddle up the reservoir leads to a boat-in campground with 17 tent sites and no roads or trails beyond.

Many campgrounds that appear remote on a map look disappointingly like RV parks once you get there. Not this one. McKenzie Ranger District personnel say this first come, first served campground gets little use.

There is also a campground on Trail Bridge Reservoir if you arrive too late to paddle into the Smith Reservoir camp. The Smith launch site has no camping.

As for the paddling, this reservoir offers a straight shot north for two miles, with deer, elk, bull trout (catch and release only), and rainbow trout among the wildlife most commonly seen from the water.

Though ranger district personnel say the water levels don't fluctuate much, I always hesitate to talk about landings on a reservoir, as the ones I saw on my trip may be under water when you're there. Plan on a 2-mile paddle with no stops.

The drive itself deserves mention. The trip along the Santiam River is a pretty one, and the vehicle climb up the gravel road from Trail Bridge to Smith Reservoir has many switchbacks that scale the side of the dam.

Other attractions: The lake is close to the city of Sisters, so drive in for one of their annual events. Among them, the rodeo in June, the quilt show in July, the Antique Faire in August, and the Folk Festival or High Mountains Jazz at Sisters Festival in September.

Suttle Lake

Maps and charts: Oregon state map.

Access: Launch at public campgrounds, Blue Bay, South Shore, or Link Creek, on the east side of the lake or at Suttle Lake Resort on the northeast end of the lake.

Mileage: Approximately 15 miles west of Sisters, 140 miles east of Portland.

Motors: 10 mph speed limit on the east end of the lake

Directions: From I-5, take US 20 in Albany heading east. Turn into Suttle Lake beyond the junction of SR 22 and US 20. Take SR 22 from I-5 in Salem as an alternate route, then continue on US 20 until you reach the lake.

More information: US Forest Service Sisters Ranger District, (541) 549-7700.
National Recreation Reservation Service, (camping reservations), (877) 444-6777.
Sisters Area Chamber of Commerce, (541) 549-0251.
Hoodoo Recreation Service, (541) 822-3799.
Suttle Lake Resort, (541) 595-6662.

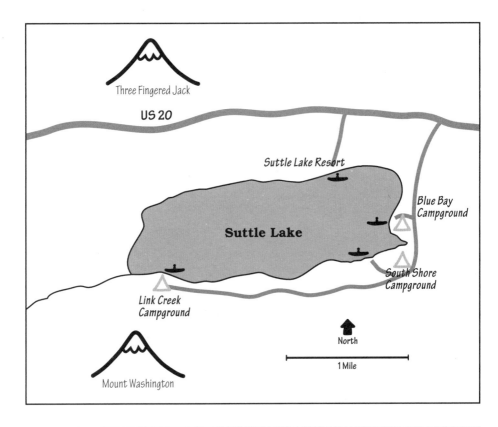

Rating: Beginner

Suttle Lake is in the foreground of Mount Washington to the south and Three Fingered Jack to the north. It is too small to be a destination paddling spot on its own, but consider adding this serene paddle onto a camping/fishing trip or weekend getaway in Central Oregon.

Sunsets in the early fall, before the cold sets in, are unbeatable times for paddling. Then plan to dine dock-side at Suttle Lake Resort's Boathouse Restaurant.

If you don't have your own boat, you can rent canoes, paddle boats, rowboats, and motorboats by the hour or by the day at the Suttle Lake Resort Marina. If demand is high enough, they could eventually add kayaks to their rental fleet. I know they've considered it.

Bald eagle, deer, otter, as well as kokanee, german browns, and rainbow trout, thrive in the area. Don't forget your binoculars for the views and gloves for those cool alpine evenings.

Camping options include the resort and three US Forest Service campgrounds in the Sisters Ranger District. The campgrounds do not have hookups, keeping the major RV element out of the camping mix. Also, you can leave your boat in the water at the campgrounds, which is always a plus.

Other attractions: Don't overlook the area in winter for snowmobile rides, cross country skiing, and snowshoeing from your cabin door.

Sisters has several annual events including Starry Nights concert series, quilt festival, rodeo and more. Check with the local chamber of commerce.

Sparks Lake

Maps and charts: Three Sisters Wilderness Area map, Oregon state map, US Forest Service Deschutes National Forest map.

Access: Launch at the day use area in the Sparks Lake Campground up Forest Service Road #400.

Or, launch on the north end of the lake just off SR 46, Cascade Lakes Highway, by taking the first left beyond Green Lakes Trail parking lot and going a short distance down the dirt road to the campground at the northern end of the lake.

Mileage: 20 miles west of Bend, 170 miles east of Portland. Lake mileage: 2 miles long.

Motors: 10 mph.

Directions: Follow US 97 toward Bend, and follow signs through downtown. Exit toward Mount Bachelor. This is the Cascade Lakes Highway, SR 46. Signs near Bend say you are on Century Drive, rather than giving road numbers, and other signs direct you toward Mount Bachelor.

More information: Bend/Fort Rock Ranger District, (541) 383-4000.
High Lake Contractors (re. camping), (541) 382-9443.
Mount Bachelor Ski and Summer Resort, (800) 829-2442.
Bend Chamber of Commerce, (800) 905-2363.
Bend Outdoor Center (boat rentals), (541) 389-7191.

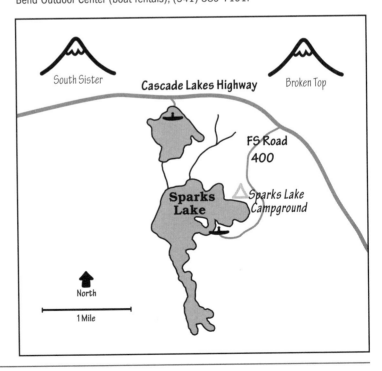

Rating: Beginner

I hesitate to give too much information about the lake size, as this is a disappearing lake, filling in with marsh flora in summer. The lake is also known to be 3 feet shallower in late summer than in spring, when snowmelt fills it again. The lake encompasses somewhere between 250-400 acres, is gorgeous, with views of South Sister, Broken Top, and Mount Bachelor, and is also the closest lake to Bend along the Cascade Lakes Highway loop.

A Northwest Forest Pass is required for most parking, but you can get one on-site in the Sparks Lake Campground.

Expect to share the lake with many fly-fishermen, as this is a popular fly-fishing-only lake.

Also expect to share the lake with wildlife. Once, in mid-September, I found myself alone, eye-to-eye with a family of common mergansers, one of the predominant waterfowl in the area. I also saw an osprey nest, and deer near the campground. With an 8 foot maximum lake depth, eagle feed here too.

The elevation at Sparks Lake is relatively high, 5,400 or more feet, so dress warmly if you've come to camp. Being a Central Oregon alpine lake, the daytime temperature often shoots into the 80s or 90s in the summer, and drops by 40 degrees most nights.

Other attractions: Mount Bachelor, Sun River, and Bend are all close by with plenty of golfing, hiking, fishing, and river rafting. Mount Bachelor has summer sightseeing, chairlift rides, interpretive tours, and mountain biking. You can eat lunch at the Mount Bachelor mile-high Scapolo's Italian Bistro barbecue from around July 4th through Labor Day, by taking the Pine Marten Express chairlift up the mountain. Mount Bachelor's annual Twilight Dinner, held over Labor Day weekend, is popular, but often sells out months in advance and requires reservations.

Elk Lake

Maps and charts: US Forest Service Deschutes National Forest map, Three Sisters Wilderness map, USGS topographic series, Elk Lake Quadrangle map, Oregon state map.

Access: There are several put-ins, including all the marked campgrounds and viewpoints on the map, and the Elk Lake Resort, where canoe rentals are available.

Mileage: 27 miles from Bend, 180 miles from Portland. Lake mileage: Less than 2 miles.

Motors: 10 mph maximum boat speed. No jet skis.

Directions: From Bend, follow signs to Mount Bachelor, on Century Drive. Marked on maps as Highway 46, signs call the road Century Drive, then Cascade Lakes Highway. The first road into Elk Lake, just before you reach Elk Lake resort, takes you around the east side of the lake, and to Hosmer Lake, as well.

Alternatively, stay on Highway 46, turning in at Elk Lake Resort, Point Campground, Beach Campground (now day-use only), or turn in to Elk Lake Loop Road, Forest Service Road #4625, at the south end of the lake, beyond Beach Campground, to get to Sunset View or other points on the eastern shore.

More information: Elk Lake Resort, (541) 480-7228.
High Lakes Contractors, (541) 382-9443.
Deschutes National Forest headquarters, (541) 388-2715.

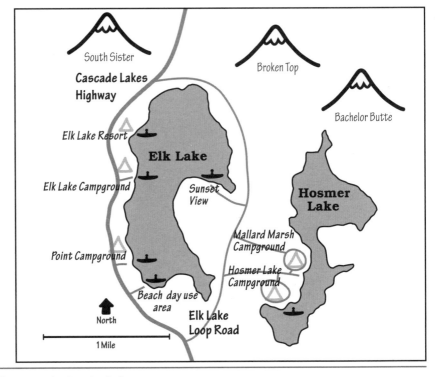

Rating: Beginner

Elk Lake is a bit exposed, making for great views of South Sister, Broken Top, and Mount Bachelor, but making paddling difficult at times. It is no wonder that this is a popular spot to sail.

Still, in early morning or at dusk, when winds generally die down, paddling here turns from wind-thrashing to calm.

Given the name, I was surprised to hear an employee at the resort say she'd never seen an elk in the area, though she added that some people have. The lake gets plenty of use, so perhaps the elk are just shy.

The resort's cabins are not on the water, so if you're staying at the resort, you can't launch from your door. But even if you're not a guest, the lodge allows parking and launching without a fee, and has a restaurant offering everything from burgers to full-course dinners. Wine and microbrews are also available.

In case you're interested in fishing from your vessel, the major catches on the lake are brook trout, brown trout and kokanee.

Campgrounds dot the lake and are well-maintained by High Lakes Contractors. These campgrounds are generally first come, first served, though some campgrounds allow group camping reservations.

Other attractions: There are cross country ski trips and dog sled tours offered between the Mount Bachelor ski area and Elk Lake during the winter. Check out the area year-round, except when the resort closes for a short time in May and again in October.

Hosmer Lake

Maps and charts: Three Sisters Wilderness map, Oregon state map, USGS topographic series, Elk Lake Quadrangle.

Access: Launch on the southwest side of the lake.

Mileage: 180 miles from Portland. Lake mileage: Slightly less than 2 miles long.

Motors: Electric motors only.

Directions: From Bend, follow signs to Mount Bachelor on SR 46, Cascade Lakes Highway. Approximately 13 miles beyond the Mount Bachelor ski area, and beyond Elk Lake Resort, turn left onto Elk Lake Loop Road. Go right at a sign directing you to a boat launch. There is no sign mentioning Hosmer Lake until you're at the gravel launch.

More information: Camping information, High Lakes Contractors, (541) 382-9443.
Bend/Fort Rock Ranger District, (541) 383-4000.
US Forest Service Deschutes National Forest headquarters, (541) 388-2715.

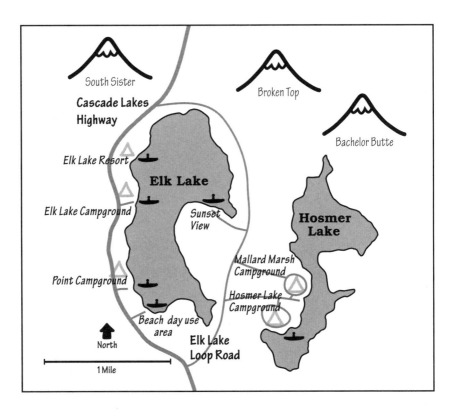

Rating: Beginner

Hosmer Lake, though encompassing only 160 acres, is the best opportunity for a quiet paddle among the Cascade Lakes, according to the locals. Hosmer is hourglass-shaped, with the connection between the two wide points on the lake being a narrow channel with ducks and other bird life in abundance. The lake looks too small to be worth taking the boat off the vehicle, until you get out there and start paddling through the reedy channel and marshes.

There are bigger lakes on the mountain, but with the shallow water and motor and fly-fishing-only restrictions, many go elsewhere. You may find serenity out on the water, even in midsummer.

In mid-September, temperatures were already dipping into the 20s at night, so plan on dressing warmly or coming in the peak summer season for the warm, dry Cascade Lakes air.

The campgrounds on Hosmer Lake are both first come, first served. Though I liked the idea of camping at Mallard Marsh Campground, because of its charming name, it truly was marshy there. The southern-most campground, near the boat launch, is the preferred campground for paddling access.

A Northwest Forest Pass is required for parking at most trailheads and is available at most resorts, including Elk Lake. However, most campgrounds have their own fees and do not require Northwest Forest Passes.

If unsure whether to purchase one, keep in mind that a pass is good in both Washington and Oregon, and for one year from the date of purchase. The funds generated from the sale of passes help maintain the forest lands, so try to think of the pass as a user-fee that is money well spent.

Other attractions: There is great hiking in the area and Bend is nearby, for your city fix.

Lava/Little Lava Lakes

Maps and charts: Three Sisters Wilderness Area map, Oregon state map, US Forest Service Deschutes National Forest map.

Access: Campground launch at the south end of Lava Lake. Lava Lake Resort launch for guests only. Little Lava Lake launch at the campground on the lake's west end.

Mileage: 45 miles from Bend. 195 miles from Portland. Lava Lake: Approximately 1.5 miles long, 300+ acres. Little Lava Lake: Approximately 1 mile perimeter.

Motors: 10 mph.

Directions: Cascade Lakes Highway to Lava Lake turn off.

More information: Crooked River Railroad Company, (541) 548-8630.
Alder Creek Kayak and Canoe, (541) 389-0890.
Bend Chamber of Commerce, (800) 905-2363.

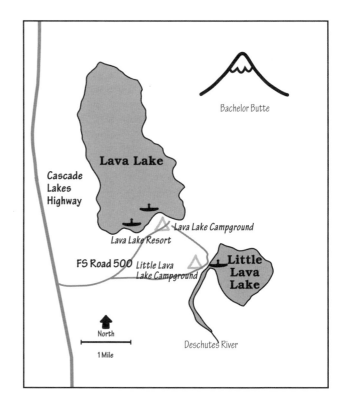

Rating: Beginner

These lakes are tiny and may not be worth the paddle unless you're already in the area checking out all the lakes, or camping at the Lava Lake Resort or campgrounds. However, with the motor restrictions, the lake remains quiet, the fishing for rainbow trout is good, I'm told, and Little Lava Lake is worth seeing, simply because it is the water source of the famous and mighty Deschutes River.

The views of surrounding peaks, Bachelor Butte and Sheridan Mountain, are beautiful and canoes are for rent at the Lava Lake Resort, making this an easy site to drive up and dip your paddle, if even for just a short time.

As for the camping, the resort was full of RV's in mid-September, so may not be what a paddler/tent camper is looking for, but the US Forest Service campgrounds, run by High Lakes Contractors, are quieter.

The reedy boat launch site at the campground beckoned me and my boat. I imagine there is tons of birdlife to see in here, especially in the early part of the summer, though I didn't see much in fall, when many migratory birds had probably already begun their southern flight.

The water on Little Lava Lake was emerald-colored. Even if you don't paddle this tiny lake, it is worth a drive-up look.

Other attractions: Bend brags of having more restaurants per capita than any other town in Oregon. From barbecue to microbrews, bakeries to bistros, take your pick after a day or weekend up at the Cascade Lakes. For a unique outing, try the Crooked River Railroad Company western-theme dinner train out of Redmond.

Cultus Lake

Maps and charts: Three Sisters Wilderness map, US Forest Service Deschutes National Forest map, Oregon state map.

Access: The main launch is at the east end of the lake at the campground, where you'll pay a small fee to park. The resort does not permit launching if you are not a guest there.

Mileage: 200 miles from Portland. 50 miles from Bend. Lake mileage: Approximately 4 miles long.

Motors: 5 mph within 200 feet of ramp, marina, or shoreline. 100 feet from any non-motorized vessel. Otherwise, this is a high-speed lake.

Directions: Go right on Century Drive in Bend, where signs point you first toward downtown, then Mount Bachelor. This is Cascade Lakes Highway, SR 46, though no signs indicate the road number. Turn right 10 miles beyond Elk Lake, where signs direct you to Cultus Lake, 50 miles from Bend.

More information: Bend/Fort Rock Ranger District, (541) 383-4000.
Cultus Lake Resort, (541) 408-1560 (summer), (800) 616-3230 (winter).

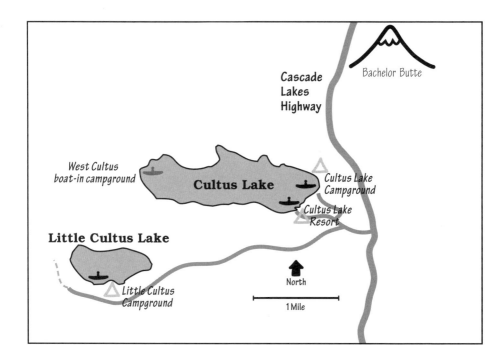

Rating: Beginner to expert

Cultus Lake is the motor-mecca lake among the Cascade Lakes. Water skiers and jet skiers tear up and down the length of the lake. Jet skis are even available for rent from the resort. Still, this is one of the bigger lakes, 785 acres, so it is a choice alpine lake for a long paddle, especially during the quieter season after Labor Day.

The resort cabins at the east end of the lake are nice, with private docks, making the lake appealing for its get-up-and-go convenience if you're staying there.

Maps show a primitive boat-in campground at the west end of the lake. While there is a campground there, it is accessible via motorboat, so it's not as isolated as I'd expected. Other campgrounds are closed for vegetation rehabilitation. Call first, if you're planning to camp in the area.

Eagle, osprey, elk, deer, ducks and geese are in the area. People coming to fish look forward to the deep lake's mackinaw and trout catch.

Views on the lake are pretty, with Cultus Butte close by to the south.

Other attractions: Little Cultus Lake is a quieter paddle, only a few miles south of Cultus Lake. When you're ready to stretch your legs, there's plenty of hiking in the area, too.

Little Cultus Lake

Maps and charts: Three Sisters Wilderness map, Oregon state map, US Forest Service Deschutes National Forest map.

Access: On the south side of the lake in the campground on Forest Service Road #4636, a launch is possible. From campsites farther up Forest Service Road # 680 on the south side of the lake, it is possible to launch from your camp.

Mileage: 200 miles from Portland. 50 miles from Bend. Lake mileage: Approximately 1.25 miles long.

Motors: 10 mph.

Directions: Follow directions to Cultus Lake, turning onto Forest Service Road #4635 toward Cultus Lake. Then turn left onto Forest Service Road #4636 directing you to Little Cultus Lake. At Little Cultus, continue beyond the boat launch sign, then veer right onto Forest Service Road #680 to farthest campsites to the west.

More information: Bend Outdoor Center, (541) 389-7191.
Powder House, (541) 389-6234.
Deschutes National Forest headquarters, (541) 388-2715.

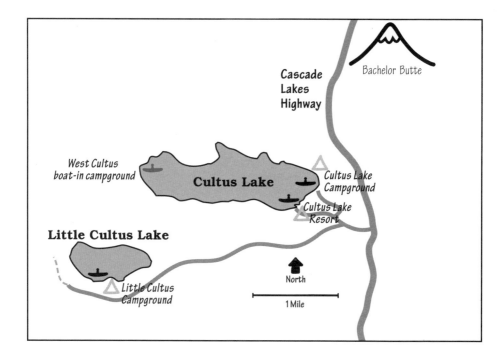

Rating: Beginner

This lake is small, only about 175 acres, but the campground up the south side of the lake is so pretty and seemingly remote that I thought the area was worth mentioning, especially as a quiet alternative to Cultus Lake, when things get crowded there.

Motoring is forbidden over 10 mph on the entire lake and fishing is restricted to fly-fishing only.

Cultus Butte, separating Cultus from Little Cultus, though relatively low, seems to pop right out of the lake.

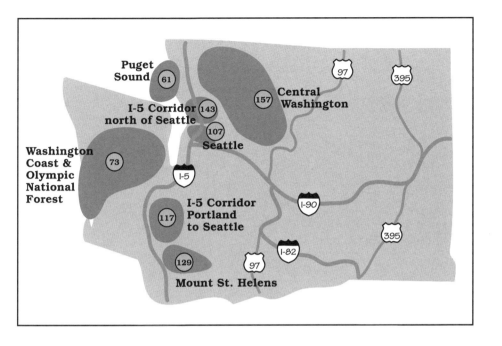

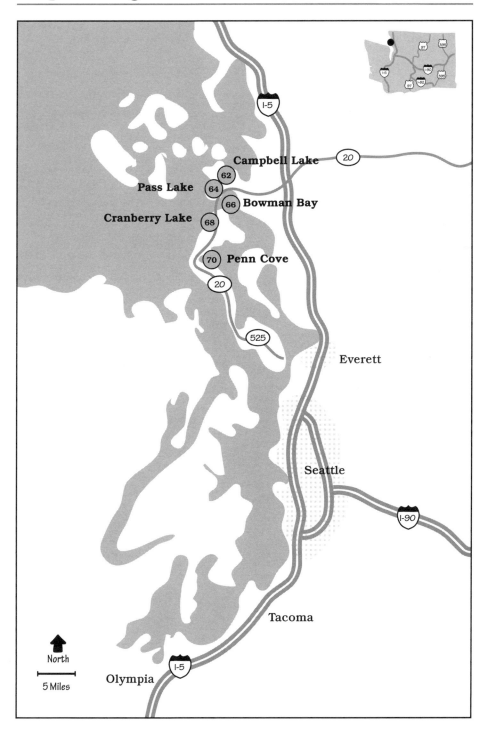

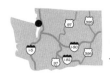

Campbell Lake

Maps and charts: Washington state map, Washington Coast map, NOAA chart #18427.

Access: Public launch off North Campbell Lake Road.

Mileage: Approximately 70 miles via SR 20 south down Fidalgo Island. Lake mileage: 1.5 miles long and 1 mile across.

Motors: No restrictions, except idling speed within 150 feet from shore.

Directions: From Seattle, go north to Mount Vernon and then west toward Anacortes on SR 20 to SR 20 south toward Deception Pass. Turn right onto North Campbell Lake Road, then left at the public fishing dock, which is also the public boat launch.

More information: Deception Pass Park, (800) 233-0321.
State Park camping reservations, (800) 452-5687.

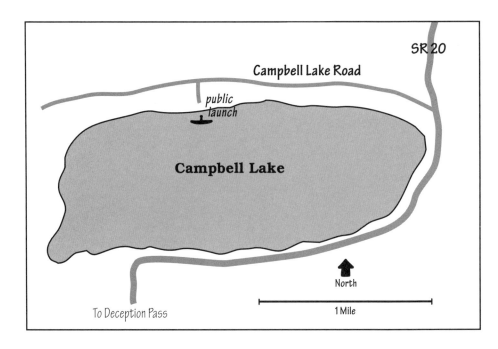

Rating: Beginner

Campbell Lake is small and serene on a weekday or in inclement weather, but a place to avoid on summer weekends, as this lake attracts jet skiers and numerous other motors. One man said he lands his floatplane on the little lake.

If you like fishing while out for a paddle, Campbell Lake has trout, yellow perch, largemouth bass, crappie, and catfish for the taking.

Aside from the one public launch, the lake is surrounded by private land.

To park at Campbell Lake, you'll need an Access Stewardship Decal, available wherever fishing and hunting licenses are sold.

No camping permitted.

Other attractions: South of Campbell Lake is the beautiful and popular Deception Pass Park for camping, hiking, more paddling, beach walks, and picnicking.

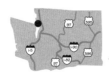

Pass Lake

Maps and charts: Washington state map, Washington Coast tour map, NOAA chart #18427.

Access: Launch just off SR 20 on Rosario Road, clearly marked to Pass Lake.

Mileage: 85 miles via Fidalgo Island and south on SR 20. Lake mileage: Close to 1 mile long.

Motors: No motors permitted.

Directions: From Seattle go north to Mount Vernon. Take SR 20 west then SR 20 south to Deception Pass. Turn right onto Rosario Road to the Pass Lake launch on the right.

More information: Washington State Park, (800) 233-0321.
State Park camping reservations, (800) 452-5687.
Deception Pass State Park, (360) 675-2417.

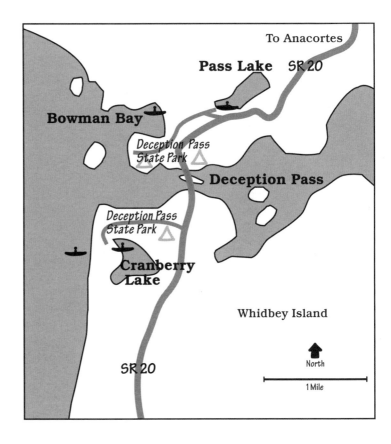

Rating: Beginner

Pass Lake is where you paddle to get away from it all. It is a small lake with no delusions of grandeur. No camping, no motors, no bait fishing — fly only. The east side runs along SR 20, which is a busy road, but the noise is muffled by the water as you paddle around the lake.

If the weather is too wild and windy for paddling anywhere else on Puget Sound, as happens often, tuck your kayak into Pass Lake.

This is an hour-long paddle or a good place to practice rolling, but not big enough to make a day of.

Other attractions: Straight across Rosario Road is the Deception Pass Park's north entrance into Bowman Bay for more paddling excitement. The camping and beach play here is primo. The campground gets very busy, but the park usually feels big enough for everyone. From coastal forest hiking to churning waters, you can have it at Deception Pass Park.

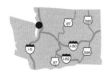

Bowman Bay (Deception Pass)

Maps and charts: Washington state map, Washington Coast tour map, NOAA chart #18427.

Access: Launch at Bowman Bay in Deception Pass State Park, north of the bridge at Deception Pass.

Mileage: Approximately 75 miles from Seattle, via Fidalgo Island.

Motors: Virtually no restrictions.

Directions: Go north from Seattle to Mount Vernon. Take SR 20 toward Anacortes, then SR 20 heading south to Deception Pass Park. Turn right on Rosario Road and left into the park.

More information: Washington State Park information, (800) 233-0321.
Camping reservations, (800) 452-5687.
Deception Pass Adventure Center kayak tours and rentals, (877) 568-6877.
Deception Pass Park information, (360) 675-2417.

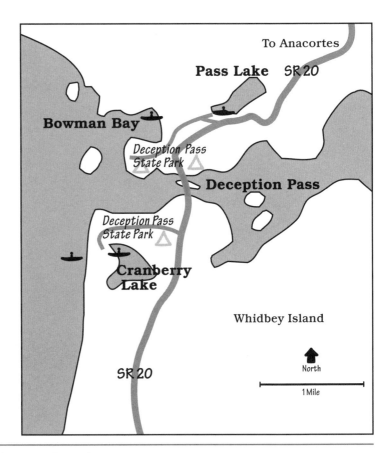

Rating: Beginner to expert

The only reason this area is rated for beginners as well as more experienced paddlers is because there are guided tours led from here. Three tours a day make a short paddle for beginners fit easily into any visitor's schedule.

But if you venture outside the protection of the bay, do so only with care and experience. Paddling northward out of the bay you quickly get into potentially rough waters. You can tuck in past Rosario Head and into Rosario Bay, but northward toward Burrows and Allan Islands, there are no landings and you're naked to the Rosario Strait. Southward from Bowman Bay can be worse. Deception Pass itself is one of the most treacherous passes in the islands. Advanced kayaking classes are taught out there.

Once warned, I can rave about the experience. Play the currents in your favor and cruise northward a good piece from Bowman Bay, and ride it back the other way for a long day trip. Being on the ocean, outside a small bay and into a strait, is exhilarating.

Once in Burrows Bay, the rock cliffs around Allan and Burrows islands are rich with anemones and sea stars, fun to float along and ponder.

If you make it that far and you need to land, you're just a leap from Washington Park, which is an easy gravel beach landing. You can camp at Washington Park, making a two-day paddle of it, if you can't reasonably catch the currents in your favor in both directions on the same day.

Other attractions: The entire Deception Pass Park is impressive. Hike forestland or beachfront. On the Whidbey Island side of Deception Pass, drive down to quaint, historic Coupeville.

Cranberry Lake

Maps and charts: Washington state map, Washington Coast tour map, NOAA chart #18427.

Access: Launch on the northwest end of Cranberry Lake, at Deception Pass Park. Once in the park, head toward West Beach camping area. No fees unless camping.

Mileage: 75+ miles from Seattle, via SR 20 south down Fidalgo Island.

Motors: Electric motors only.

Directions: From Mount Vernon, take SR 20 west toward Anacortes, then SR 20 south down Fidalgo Island. Cross the bridge near Deception Pass and turn into the state park south entrance on Whidbey Island. Stop for the very helpful map at the entrance booth, though you needn't pay unless you're staying the night.

More information: Washington State Park information, (800) 233-0321.
Washington State Park camping reservations, (800) 452-5687.
Deception Pass Park, (360) 675-2417.
Anacortes visitor information, (360) 293-3832.
Deception Pass Adventure Center kayak rentals and tours,
(877) 568-6877.

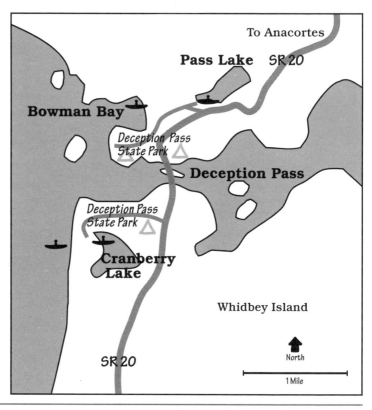

Rating: Beginner

Cranberry Lake is small, calm and shallow, and perfect for a family paddle with youngsters. Across from the boat launch is a boat rental shop, in case you didn't bring your own vessel.

The lake is so close to the ocean that you feel the ocean air, while paddling the quiet lake waters.

The pond lilies give the lake a swampy feel in late summer. There is nothing more relaxing than a slow paddle on a hot fall afternoon.

Deception Pass Park, with its hiking trails and beaches, is fabulous, but popular in summer. Therefore, this is an excellent place to be *after* Labor Day. Also, there are fewer late afternoon winds in fall, so the possibility of graduating into the ocean at Bowman Bay (the north entrance to Deception Pass Park on Fidalgo Island) or other bay paddles off Whidbey and Fidalgo Islands, is better then.

Other attractions: We've always enjoyed the summer street fair in nearby Anacortes, just north of the lakes. There is a handmade, kid-sized, functional railway that shuttles families through and around town, making this fair memorable and unique. The locals know how to do it up for this event.

Penn Cove

Maps and charts: Washington state map, NOAA chart #18423.

Access: Recommended launches are on the south side of the cove. Launch from the public park landing in Coupeville or the end of Marine Drive onto Long Point. Second choice, launch at Monroe Landing on the north shore. To get there follow the shoreline around the lake on Madrona Way to Penn Cove Road. It was very slippery when I was there — be careful.

In Oak Harbor, launch at Beeksma Gateway Park, on Beeksma Drive, but only at high tide. This area is sunken in mudflats at low tide — no place to be trying to drag a kayak ashore. It looked shoe-sucking thick.

Mileage: Approximately 75 miles northwest of Seattle, including mileage over water via ferry.

Motors: No restrictions but jet skiers are not prevalent according to the Oak Harbor Marina personnel. I didn't see any on the water.

Directions: From Seattle go to Whidbey Island either via the Mukilteo ferry or around through Anacortes and down Fidalgo Head. Either south down SR 20 or north up SR 525, once in Coupeville, launch on Ninth Street at Captain Thomas Coupe Park. Ninth Street turns into Parker Road east of town.

More information: Penn Cove Water Festival, (360) 679-7391.
Central Whidbey Chamber of Commerce, (360) 678-5434.
State Parks information, (800) 233-0321.
Statewide reservations, (800) 452-5687.
Washington State Ferry information, (800) 843-3779.

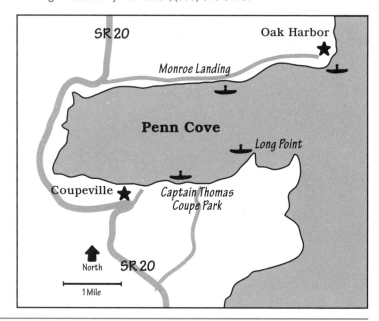

Rating: Beginner to expert

Penn Cove is a good place for beginning paddlers to safely head out on the ocean, unguided. The reason is that you can follow the shoreline with long stretches of beach and land anywhere you need to. There are many areas with private homes or tidelands, but emergency landings throughout the bay are possible.

Though the cove is also fairly protected, compared to the open east or west side of Whidbey Island, expect winds most afternoons. As usual, the best times to paddle here are mornings and evenings.

When I was there, eagles circled over the mouth of the cove near Long Point, and I saw pidgeon guillomots, seal, and otter. The area is known for its mussels and clam digging. Crabbing is good too, according to locals. Licenses are required.

Though you need to ferry, it is possible to do this paddle after a day's work in Seattle. Commuter traffic gets high, but the ferries, running every half-hour, keep the cars moving pretty well. We only had a 30 minute wait on a mid-July Friday evening. The cove is worth a day trip, but if you have longer, Whidbey Island and Fidalgo Head to the north are rich in paddling sites (see Cranberry, Pass and Campbell lakes, and Bowman Bay).

Other attractions: Coupeville has an annual Concerts on the Cove series and a water festival with Native American canoe races and other water activities.

The town is attractive and the Great Times Espresso shop, where a sign reads, "Loitering Encouraged," was a great stop after a day paddle — strong, hot coffee, a reading nook, baked goods, and endless java aroma.

Finally, just in case you want to spend outdoor time doing things other than paddling, Coupeville has a rich history and hiking trails, including Ebey's Landing, where you can also put in a kayak on the beach, though into sometimes wilder waters on the west side of Whidbey Island.

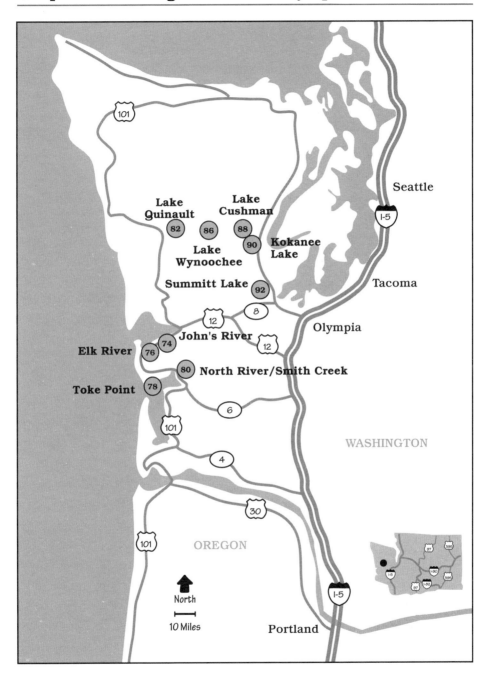

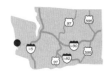

John's River

Maps and Charts: NOAA chart #18502, Metzger's Gray's Harbor County map, Washington state map.

Access: One launch in Markham, 12 miles down SR 105 south from Aberdeen. US Fish and Wildlife Access Stewardship Decal required and available where hunting/fishing licenses are sold.

Mileage: 180 miles from Portland. 125 miles from Seattle. 60 miles from Olympia. Paddling miles: Unlimited.

Motors: Few boats go up river; Most go out into Gray's Harbor.

Directions: Take I-5 to SR 12 and head west toward Aberdeen. From Aberdeen, follow signs to SR 105, heading south toward Westport. 12 miles down SR 105, turn left onto John's River Road, just past the bridge over John's River. Turn left from John's River Road to Game Farm Road, to the US Fish and Wildlife Department parking area.

More information: Washington State Department of Fish and Wildlife, Wildlife Program (hunting schedules), (360) 902-2515.
Westport/Grayland Chamber of Commerce, (800) 345-6223.
Skookum Bay Outfitters (paddling information and rentals), (360) 533-0825.
Friends of Gray's Harbor — FOGH— (Shorebird Festival information and ecological information), (360) 648-2254.

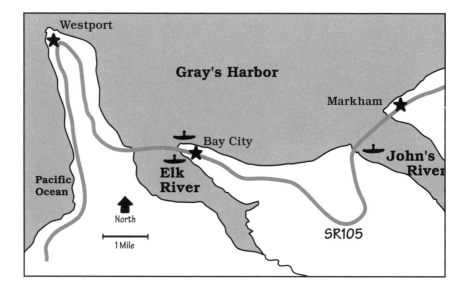

Rating: Beginner to expert

I won't try to hide my bias — I love this area. But it becomes a nightmare during hunting season. Call for a hunting schedule and avoid the noise, anxiety, and potential danger of paddling near duck hunters.

When I've paddled the John's River, I've found the launch bustling with friendly fishermen, but rarely do they go up the John's River. Instead, they head out to Gray's Harbor. Near the launch, it's noisy with cars, boats, and construction equipment near the highway. But, paddling up the river, the offensive clatter quickly subsides, until the only sounds you hear are reedy marsh grasses blowing and the occasional splash of breaching salmon. Once I had a silent harbor seal escort swimming in front of my boat all day, looking back occasionally, as if checking to be sure I was still following.

With regard to wildlife, you may see fox, elk, deer, cormorants, and ducks of many kinds. Overhead, bald eagles circle and fish.

The paddle is protected well from wind unless you head out onto the open Gray's Harbor. Be careful out there.

This river is tidal, so plan carefully. I like to paddle up river at slack, before ebb, or at the tail end of the flood tide, then ride the river back to the launch on the strong ebbing tide. It is a cruise back, if you time it just right.

The only drawback to the area is the sleeping accommodations. Camping at Twin Harbors State Park is possible along the beach side, but the area is popular and none too private. Across Gray's Harbor are more upscale, condo-type accommodations in Ocean Shores, and the nearby coastal towns of Grayland and Westport have small motels near the waterfront. I prefer the historic Tokeland Hotel, a bit farther down the road in Tokeland, because of its simple tidiness and old-fashioned feel. Aberdeen area has bed and breakfast possibilities, as well.

Other attractions: Plenty to do, including summer art festivals, chainsaw carving contests, surfing contests, the Elk River Challenge boat races, and Spring's Shorebird Festival in Hoquiam. The fall Cranberry Harvest Festival and winter/spring whale-watching tours round out the year with tourist activities. You can also check out a deep-sea fishing excursion from Westport, if you've never been.

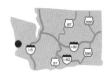

Elk River

Maps and charts: NOAA chart #18502, Washington state map, Metzger's Gray's Harbor county map.

Access: Launch down Whaler Road at the hunt club, by permission only, or launch from Brady's Oyster Farm, where it is also courteous to ask permission to park.

Mileage: 185 miles from Portland. Paddling mileage: Unlimited.

Motors: More boats head out into Gray's Harbor than up the river, except during hunting season.

Directions: Take I-5 to SR 12 west toward Aberdeen. From Aberdeen, follow signs to SR 105 south toward Westport. Before Westport, in Bay City, turn right into Brady's Oyster Farm or left on Whalebone Way to Whalers Street. Follow it down to the hunt club ramp and ask permission to use the private launch.

More information: Brady's Oyster Farm, (360) 268-0077.
Washington State Department of Fish and Wildlife, Wildlife Program (hunting schedules), (360) 902-2515.
Westport/Grayland Chamber of Commerce, (800) 345-6223.
Skookum Bay Outfitters (paddling information and rentals), (360) 533-0825.
Friends of Gray's Harbor – FOGH– (Shorebird Festival information and ecological information), (360) 648-2254.

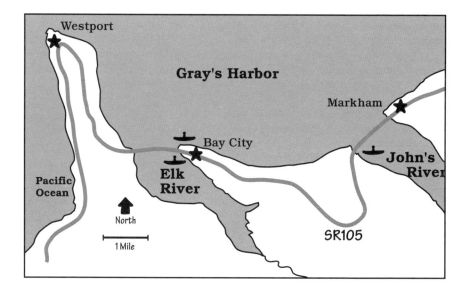

Rating: Beginner to intermediate

Elk River is an expansive estuary. My opinion of the area is tainted by the fact that I first went there on the opening day of duck hunting season, in pouring rain, in October. It was loud, wet, cold and crowded. I needed a sign and a red beacon on my head to show that "Yikes, I'm not a duck!" Call me overly cautious, but something about men, guns and camouflage clothes makes me nervous.

At any rate, the river is beautiful any other time of year, and many enjoy it during the famous July Elk River Challenge boat race.

This river is tidal, so plan accordingly. Try not to find yourself upriver at the peak of flood tide, trying to paddle back to the launch. It's a tough workout. Conversely, riding the flood upriver and the ebb back to the launch is a breeze.

Look for seal, an occasional elk or fox along the banks, ducks, geese, eagle, heron, and cormorant, of course.

For launching, the county road ends at Brady's Oyster Farm. The launch there isn't optimal and I felt a bit intrusive. It is nice to stop in at the retail store and ask permission to launch, though the land is public, according to Brady.

Similarly, down the road off Whalebone Way, the launch is owned by a hunt club. They generally don't mind you parking and paddling from here, if it is not hunting season. However, this is a private launch, so ask first, if anyone is around to talk with.

Other attractions: Brady's Oyster Feed is a fun benefit worth spending some money on. In the past, the proceeds have gone to clean water promotion and college scholarship funds.

The area is booming with seasonal activities including the spring Shorebird Festival, art fairs, parades, fishing derbies, Cranberry Harvest Festival, kite festivals, and surf and paddling contests.

Toke Point

Maps and charts: NOAA chart #18504, Washington state map.

Access: Toke Point public dock in Tokeland on the northwest side of Willapa Bay.

Mileage: 160 miles from Portland or Seattle.

Motors: Virtually unrestricted.

Directions: From points south of Willapa Bay, take I-5 north to SR 6 in Chehalis. Follow SR 6 west to Raymond, then take US 101 over the Willapa River, then SR 105 north to Tokeland. Turn left following signs to Tokeland on Tokeland Road. This turns into Kindred Road. Turn left on Third Avenue and follow it around to the Toke Point dock on Emerson Road. Or, take Kindred Road to North Street, turn left on North Street, then right onto Emerson to Toke Point.

From Seattle, take Exit #104 toward Highway 101 and Aberdeen. From Aberdeen, follow signs to SR 105 south, following SR 105 to Tokeland.

Or, take SR 107 south from Montesano, then US 101 south toward Raymond, turning on SR 105 to Tokeland.

A good state map is helpful with all the loops around Gray's Harbor and Willapa Bay.

More information: Tokeland Hotel, (360) 267-7006.
Westport/Grayland Chamber of Commerce, (800) 345-6223.
US Fish and Wildlife Montesano office, (360) 249-4628.

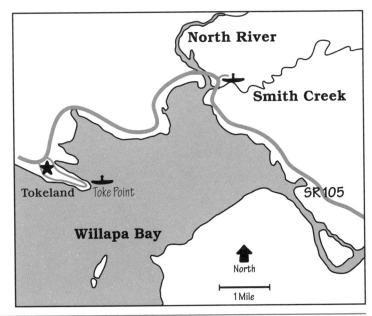

Rating: Expert

Willapa Bay is beautiful, but also quite exposed. At low tide the expansive mudflats make landing your boat for a pit stop difficult, too. But when the winds are calm, Willapa Bay is the place to paddle to see shorebirds. Just standing at the Toke Point launch you'll see sandpiper, snipe, gull, tern, and maybe oyster catcher, pelican, and duck.

If you want to paddle in the area, consider having an alternative plan in case you encounter windy conditions. See the North River/Smith Creek section for a nearby alternative launch with more protection during inclement weather.

At Toke Point, fishermen were friendly and fun to talk with about their days catch.

During certain times of year, gill netters make paddling here treacherous, as their nets span large areas on the water. Don't get scooped up — both you and the fishermen will be unhappy. Caution: these fishermen are working. Assume that you haven't been spotted and stay clear of fishing vessels.

Other attractions: Can't think of a thing to do here except clamming, crabbing, beachcombing, whale watching, visiting the cranberry fields, shopping for woodcarvings, or fishing. Your choices, on and off the water, are plentiful.

North River/Smith Creek

Maps and charts: NOAA chart #18504, Washington state map.

Access: One launch on Smith Creek, which accesses Smith Creek, North River, and Willapa Bay. Access Stewardship Decal required and available where hunting and fishing licenses are sold (most nearby hardware stores).

Mileage: 60 miles from Chehalis, 150 miles from Portland, 160 miles from Seattle. Unlimited paddling distances including North River, Smith Creek, and Willapa Bay.

Motors: River and creek are shallow enough at low tide to keep high-speed boaters out.

Directions: Take SR 6 heading west from Chehalis. In Raymond, take US 101 over the Willapa River, then SR 105 north just past milepost 10. Take the first right after the Smith Creek Bridge, into the public parking lot and launch on Smith Creek.

More information: Tokeland Hotel, (360) 267-7006.
Gray whale charters or other Gray's Harbor information, (800) 473-6018.
US Fish and Wildlife Montesano Office, (360) 249-4628.

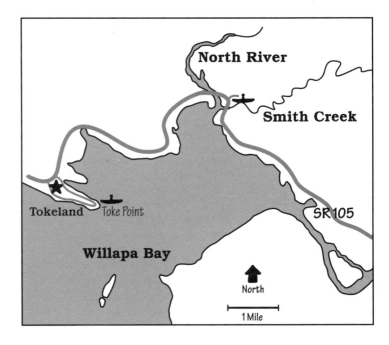

Rating: Beginner to expert

Smith Creek/North River is a great choice for launching around the Willapa Bay area, because the options in here are numerous. If it is windy, you can quietly paddle up North River or Smith Creek, and if it is calm, you can treat yourself to a Willapa Bay paddle.

At either place, with some planning, you can see harbor seals and shorebirds, smell the ocean air, and have a safe coastal kayaking experience, even as a relative beginner.

If you don't feel confident in your rolling, bracing, or self-rescue skills, stay along the shoreline in Willapa Bay, or paddle along the rivers, because, like any coastal paddle, the winds can come up without warning and turn the calm estuary into a churning washing machine.

To paddle the North River, launch on Smith Creek and head out toward Willapa Bay instead of up the creek. Turn right once in the bay, under the North River Bridge, up the North River.

I like to start this paddle at high tide, just before the ebb. That way, I am paddling up river against the current, then riding that current back on the ebb's full force a few hours later. Ideally, paddling up river during high tide, then turning around at slack water, letting the current flush you back out toward the bay, is perfect. However, if timing doesn't allow for this, it is always best to paddle against the current first, and with it on the return trip, when you're tired.

I love this area and see sandpiper, snipe, oyster catcher, crab, salmon, and seal on every trip. Seal seem to hang out at the mouths of rivers and bays, waiting for food to float by with the current.

On the open Willapa Bay, it is also possible to see whale, brown pelican, and nesting seagull and tern on the mudflats.

Other attractions: Tokeland and Raymond are both nearby. I fell in love with the historic Tokeland Hotel, with its tiny rooms with quilt-laden beds, old-fashioned feel, and its dining and sitting rooms. It's a cozy place to be on a rainy afternoon or after paddling, clamming, or sightseeing from Willapa Bay to Gray's Harbor.

In early July, Tokeland hosts a big parade and celebration and in November, the hotel's annual arts and crafts fair is a benefit event for the Children's Hospital in Seattle. In Gray's Harbor, just north of Tokeland, check out whale watching tours March-May.

Lake Quinault

Maps and charts: Washington state map, US Forest Service Olympic National Forest map.

Access: Launch possible from four campgrounds around the lake, three on South Shore Road and one on North Shore Road. Launching is also free and easy at Lake Quinault Resort and Lake Quinault Lodge, even if you are not a guest.

Mileage: Approximately 200 miles from Seattle and 225 miles from Portland. The lake is approximately 5 miles long and 2 miles across.

Motors: 24 mph speed limit. No jet skis or water skiing allowed.

Directions: From I-5 heading south from Seattle, take Exit #104 in Olympia (Aberdeen-Ocean Beaches) and go west through Aberdeen to Hoquiam. In Hoquiam, head north on US 101, 40 miles to Lake Quinault. Turn right onto South Shore Road or North Shore Road, soon after.

From 1-5 north from Portland, take US 12 West, near Centralia. Stay on US 12 to Hoquiam and take US 101 north 40 miles to Lake Quinault.

More information: Lake Quinault Lodge boat rentals, dining and room reservations, (800) 562-6672.
Lake Quinault Resort rooms and boat tours but no boat rentals, (800) 650-2362.
Quinault's Rain Forest Resort Village. Home to the world's largest spruce tree, cabin rentals, lakeside RV park and canoe rentals, (800) 255-6936.
Olympic National Forest Quinault office for campground information on the south side of the lake, (360) 288-2525.
Olympic National Park (north side of the lake), (360) 288-2444.

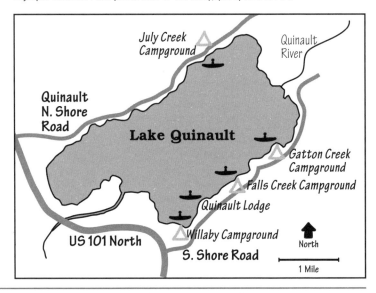

Rating: Beginner to expert

Lake Quinault is in the Olympic National Forest — the temperate rainforest. Thus, it rains a lot there. But, a kayak is a good place to be in the rain, because, spray-skirted in, you can stay fairly dry.

Heavy rainfall gives rise to enormous trees around the lake and mild weather — usually 50-70 degrees. Also thanks to the heavy rainfall, the area looks painted in every shade of green, year-round.

On the west end of the lake, there is a fish hatchery and fish farm to paddle by. The east end of the lake is farther from the noise of Highway 101, has reeds and channels to paddle up and the Quinault River to explore, if you're a strong enough paddler to head upstream. Since the wind usually comes from the west, if you're on the east end of the lake after noon, you can count on a good workout paddling upwind, unless you parked at either Gatton Creek or July Creek campgrounds on the southeast and northeast sides of the lake.

If you get caught in strong winds, some shelter is possible paddling close to shore. Unless you want to practice your bracing, rolling, or rescue skills, avoid the middle of the lake when those afternoon winds come up. Whitecaps and waves can kick up quickly and are surprisingly large for a lake environment.

The lake is full of salmon, Dolly Varden, and trout. Tribal fishing permits are required and available at most stores around the lake.

Wildlife abounds. We saw eagle, loon, beaver, and osprey. As for the surrounding flora on land, trillium, ferns of every kind, Oregon oxalis, salmonberry, moss, and mushrooms are just a few things you'll find when you get out of the boat for a walk in the woods.

On sunny days, the view of the snow-capped and majestic Olympic Mountains is unbeatable, but for most of the winter, spring and fall clouds obstruct the views.

My favorite launch spot is the Lake Quinault Lodge, for several reasons. Because the lodge is halfway up the lake, you can launch and paddle in either direction, depending on the weather.

Because the best paddling times are

mornings and evenings, the lodge offers great lunchtime picnic and play opportunities, with an extensive lawn area, complete with horseshoe pits and volleyball courts, or a luxury lunch in the lodge dining room.

Another reason I like launching at the lodge is that the staff, especially at the boat dock where they rent kayaks, canoes, paddle and rowboats, is extremely helpful and friendly.

Also near the lodge, there are several hiking trails, should you care to land and take a walk.

Finally, okay, say it's raining. Nothing beats curling up with a drink around the huge fireplace in the lobby/lounge after a day's paddle.

The campgrounds are all first come, first served. Willaby, Falls Creek, and Gatton Creek are all Olympic National Forest campgrounds, while the July Creek campground is under Olympic National Park jurisdiction.

Other attractions: The ocean beaches are within 20 miles for beach play, Lake Quinault Lodge has an indoor pool and game room for kids, the US Forest Service offers ranger-led interpretive programs in the summer, and rainforest hikes are plentiful on well-maintained trails throughout the area. Sol Duc Hotsprings is up the road to the north and there's gourmet food with a view in a casual atmosphere at the Quinault Lodge and other restaurants in the area.

Wynoochee Lake

Maps and charts: Olympic National Forest and National Park maps, Washington state map.

Access: Coho Campground on the south end of the lake.

Mileage: 200 miles from Portland, 120 miles from Seattle, 60 miles from Olympia. Lake mileage: 6-plus miles long.

Motors: No-wake zone near boat launch.

Directions: From I-5 take US 101 to SR 8 toward Aberdeen. Just beyond the town of Montesano, take a right (north) on Wynoochee Valley Road (which become Forest Service Road #22) for 35 miles to the Coho Campground. The road is unpaved for the last 20 miles. No services are available, so be sure to have plenty of gas for the 70-mile round trip.

More information: Hood Canal Ranger Station, (360) 877-5254.
Tacoma Public Utilities (water level information) (888) 502-8690.

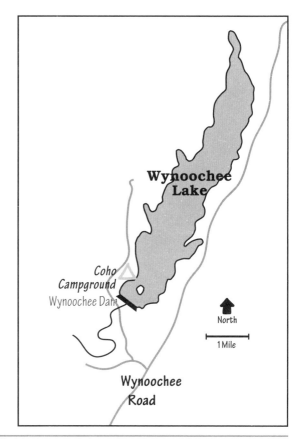

Rating: Beginner to expert

Wynoochee Lake does not share the pristine wilderness atmosphere of the nearby Quinault area, and is, frankly, a motorist's dream, and not the best place for paddling on crowded summer weekends.

There is heavy logging in the area that creates unattractive clearcuts, and when water flows are down, dreary stumps and high dirt banks detract from the shoreline ambiance. You can inquire about water levels before you go though, by contacting the Tacoma Public Utilities.

Negatives aside, when motor use is down on weekdays, or in the spring and fall, you can get a good workout paddle in on this large lake.

The Coho Campground is available on a first come, first served basis, but the camp host said that even when the campground is full, they generally find a spot for anyone that makes the drive.

Eagle, osprey, deer, cougar, and bear are a few of the creatures you might encounter.

Other attractions: Not far from the rainforest to the west and Hood Canal to the east, there are plenty of opportunities for other paddles, or a nice meal in either direction from the lake. There is a 12-mile loop trail around Wynoochee Lake for hikers, but I recommend stopping for a detailed map of the area before heading out, as there are many old roads crisscrossing the region.

The Wynoochee Dam is near the campground and also worth a visit if you want to slip in a physical science and engineering lesson.

Lake Cushman

Maps and charts: US Forest Service Olympic National Forest map, Olympic National Park map, Washington state map.

Access: Lake Cushman State Park approximately a third of the way up the east shore of the lake. Launch fee required. Alternatively, you can launch for a fee, even if not a patron, at Lake Cushman Resort, near the southeast end of the lake, 3 miles before the state park.

Mileage: 100 miles from Seattle, 45 miles from Olympia, 160 miles from Portland. Lake mileage: 11 miles long.

Motors: 6 mph within 100 feet of anyone else. 300 feet from boat launches and 150 feet from shoreline. No jet ski launching from the resort before 10 a.m. and after dusk.

Directions: Take I-5 to Olympia, Exit #104. Then, go north on US 101 to Hoodsport along Hood Canal. Turn left in Hoodsport on Lake Cushman Road (Highway 119) and go approximately 5 miles to the lake.

More information: Shelton-Mason County Chamber of Commerce, (800) 576-2021.
Hoodsport Information, (360) 877-9010.
Lake Cushman Resort, (800) 588-9630.
Lake Cushman State Park reservations, (800) 452-5687.

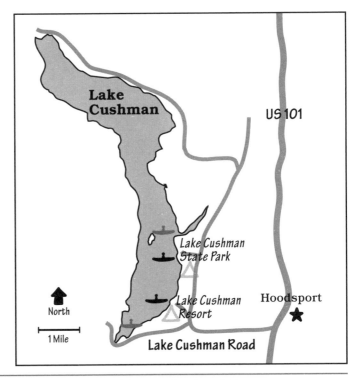

Rating: Beginner to expert

Even though motorboats and floatplanes are on the move on Lake Cushman, the lake still has surprising appeal for paddlers. On weekdays and in the off season, the lake is quiet, giving paddlers a prime opportunity to quietly enjoy the Olympic Mountains, which look like they sprout right out of the north end of the lake.

The state park and Cushman Resort have grounds for camping, and when winds pick up, as we know they do most everywhere in the Northwest on the water, you can find shelter in coves near both launches.

You can leave your boat in the water by camp at Cushman Resort, if you're staying the night, or rent a cabin on the lake at the resort and have your own private dock. Kayak, paddleboat, motorboat and jet ski rentals are available at the resort as well as the usual Washington fare — espresso.

Though much of the lake is surrounded by private homes, landings are possible at the resort, the state park, and state land on a peninsula at the south end of the lake. Across from the state park, there is a park-owned island to land and picnic on, also.

Mergansers float this lake, and you can expect to see eagle and osprey, too. On land, deer and elk roam the area. Bear and cougar sightings are also possible.

Other attractions: Hoodsport is an adorable town with a spirited annual 4th of July celebration. Shelton, 15 miles to the south, has a spring Forestfest including parades and vendors, and nearby Mason County Fair in July and Oysterfest in October.

Kokanee Lake

Maps and charts: Olympic National Forest and National Park maps, Washington state map.

Access: Public launch at the south end of the lake.

Mileage: 150 miles from Seattle, 40 miles from Olympia, 150 miles from Portland. Lake mileage: Approximately 3-mile perimeter.

Motors: 10 hp motors maximum.

Directions: Take I-5 to Exit #104 in Olympia. Go north on US 101 to Hoodsport, then left onto Cushman Road. At the Lake Cushman Grocery, turn left onto Cushman-Potlatch Road. Veer right until you get to the lake and turn left into the public access parking.

More information: Hood Canal Ranger District, (360) 877-5254.
Wilderness Information Center, (360) 452-0300.
Hoodsport area camping, lodging and services, (360) 877-9010.
Shelton -Mason County Chamber of Commerce, (800) 576-2021.

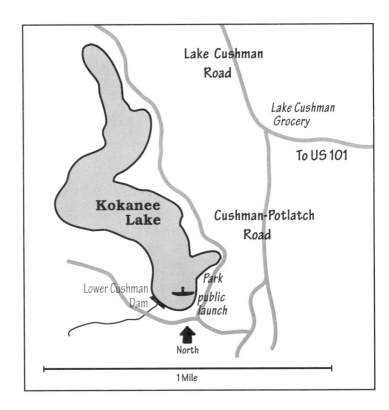

Rating: Beginner

This lake almost didn't make it into the book because of its small size, but it was too charming to leave out.

The park by the boat launch was groomed and in full bloom in September, when we visited and paddled the lake.

The Olympic Mountains make for the best backdrop in the world, in my opinion, and are visible from the launch at the south end of the lake.

Because the lake twists and almost switches back, it is much shorter as the crow flies than its actual paddling distance.

The lake sides are steep and landings few, but the sidewalls give rise to a great waterfall, three-quarters of the way up the lake.

This is an especially fine place to be, if you're looking for peace and quiet, or shelter from the wind. Close by Hood Canal gets very rough and, though enormous, isn't an option for anything but expert paddlers, most of the time. Nearby Lake Cushman gets a great deal of motorboat traffic and may be too bustling for many paddlers' tastes on summer weekends.

Wildlife in the area is abundant, including hawk and osprey. Kingfishers chatter constantly, making their presence known, too.

Except for the occasional cackling kingfisher, this lake defines quiet.

Other attractions: Hoodsport has all the standard tourist fare, including good ice cream on a hot summer day. The famous "Staircase" hiking trails into the Olympic National Park are right up the road.

Summit Lake

Maps and charts: US Forest Service Olympic National Forest map, Olympic National Park map, Washington state map.

Access: One launch site on the southwest shore. Access Stewardship Decal from US Fish and Wildlife Department required and available where hunting and fishing licenses are sold.

Mileage: Approximately 80 miles from Seattle, 15 miles from Olympia, 130 miles from Portland. Lake mileage: 2.2 miles long, less than .5 miles wide.

Motors: Maximum lake speed 45 mph. Jet skis allowed from 11:00 a.m. to dusk. Counterclockwise when going more than 5 mph.

Directions: From I-5 take US 101 to SR 8, heading toward Aberdeen. Turn right on Summit Lake Road and into the public fishing access parking lot.

More information: Olympia Chamber of Commerce, (360) 357-3362.

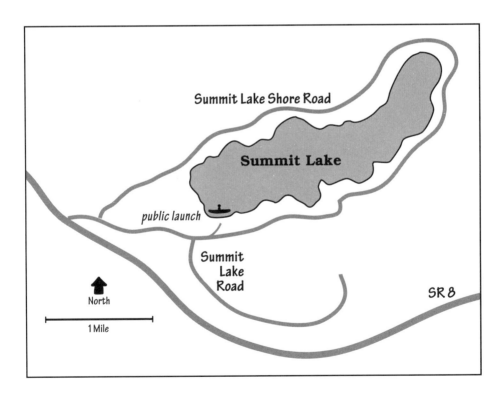

Rating: Beginner

The lakeshore is almost entirely privately owned, but there is a marsh at the west end of the lake to explore, and wildlife in the reeds.

There are kokanee and rainbow trout in these waters, and kingfisher, merganser, loon, heron, mallard, eagle, and osprey in and around the lake. River otter, raccoon, and deer also surround the area, making this a great urban escape for those from Olympia.

If you're from somewhere beyond Olympia, you might choose a paddle that is a little farther off the beaten track. Though the lake was quiet on the weekday that I visited, any place with boating regulations, including rules mandating the direction of travel on the lake, implies a bustling waterway.

Don't forget to pick up an Access Stewardship Decal, which is required at the public fishing dock and at many other parking lots in the area.

Other attractions: As Washington's state capitol, nearby Olympia is the site of many annual attractions, including Capitol City Lakefair in July, Fall Harbor Days, and a farmer's market, which sells produce, as well as arts and crafts, from Thursday through Sunday each summer. Washington also displays its creative talent at Art Walk, held each year in spring and fall.

Smith & Bybee Lakes paddle adventure.

Summer on Silver Lake.

Mount Hood view from Timothy Lake.

We'll take 80 degrees and sunny any day.

Life should always be this good!

When do I get to paddle dad?

Kendra Berry in her element on the water.

Mother/daughter sunset paddle.

Big people and little people ride the waters of Tillamook Bay.

Femmes afloat.

Toke Point on Willapa Bay.

Ross Lake Resort floating cabins.

View from Ross Lake Resort toward Ross Dam and North Cascade Glacial Peaks.

Dad prepares for retirement, while the kids do all the paddling. Diablo Lake, en route to Ross Lake.

Wings on the water.

Lacamas Lake in midsummer.

More Femmes afloat.

Looking for mussels.

There's nothing like an afternoon on the ocean.

It looks like great weather on Willapa Bay, but most of the paddling was in wind and rain. Don't EVER leave your windbreaker and pile jacket in the car!

Family paddlers and family passengers (there are those who do and those who supervise).

Morning on Puget Sound

Images from the water's edge.

Ross Lake, North Central Washington.

High Cascade Lakes, Central Oregon

Yes, the sunset is great, but we're still two miles from the take-out.

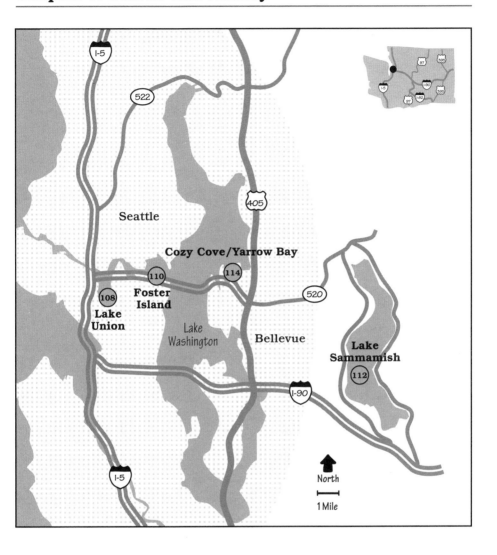

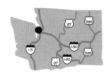

Lake Union

Maps and charts: Seattle city map. Washington Water Trails Association map.

Access: Launch east of Gas Works Park at the Sunnyside ramp, or put in at the Northwest Outdoor Center on the west end of the lake (Westlake Avenue N.). Moss Bay and Agua Verde rent boats and have access to the water on the southeast and north ends of the lake. And, there is a Seattle Parks and Recreation launch just under the I-5 bridge by the Pocock Rowing Center. There are other launches in the vicinity, usually parking being the limiting factor.

Mileage: Paddling distance: Approximately 4.5 mile perimeter, 598 acres.

Motors: 7 knots.

Directions: I-5 to Mercer, west (left) on Mercer, right on Aurora to Westlake Ave. or Northlake Way.

Alternatively, take the 45th Street exit from I-5, and go left on 45th Street to Stone Way. Take another left on Stone Way and then left on Northlake Way past Gas Works Park to the Sunnyside launch.

More information: Northwest Outdoor Center, (206) 281-9694.
Moss Bay Kayaks (southeast side by TGIF), (206) 682-2031.
Agua Verde (rentals and food on the north end of the lake), (595) 455-8570.
Seattle Parks Department, (206) 684-4075

SR 99

Sunnyside
public launch

Nickerson St.

N. Northlake Way

Gas Works Park

Fairview Ave. E.

Westlake Ave. N.

Lake Union

I-5

Moss Bay Kayaks

NWOC

SR 99

North

0.2 Miles

Fairview Ave. N.

Rating: Beginner

With seaplanes buzzing overhead, Lake Union doesn't whisper serenity most of the time. What it does offer is a relaxing urban paddle within city limits, just minutes from your office door.

It is also one of the best ways to demo boats, if you're looking to buy. The Northwest Outdoor Center (NWOC) is located on the west side of the lake and they rent boats by the day or by the hour, allowing you to come in and out for a new boat every few minutes if you want to. Not only can you try out several boats in a single day, but you can compare them under similar conditions by trying them one after the other. Demos are free to serious buyers. Moss Bay and Agua Verde both rent boats as well,

The lake is also good for practicing rescue skills or bracing in windy conditions.

The park on the north side of the lake is a Seattle favorite kite flying point, so even if you don't fly kites yourself, you can watch some amazing stunts at the ends of other's lines.

For environmental reasons, the park shoreline is closed. You cannot land, launch, or swim at Gas Works Park, though this restriction will hopefully be lifted soon. There is a public launch just east of the park.

On the south end of the lake, beware of the seaplane landing strip. While other paddlers say they've never had a problem, I have. Either observe the pattern of planes before approaching or better yet, avoid that end of the lake all together.

I think the lake's highlight is its numerous choices for paddle-in dining.

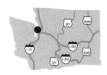

Foster Island

Maps and charts: Seattle city map.

Access: Launch at McCurdy Park on Union Bay by the 200-acre Washington Park Arboretum or across Union Bay at the University.

Motors: Area around the island is shallow and motorboats stay out in Lake Washington.

Directions: Head east on SR 520 from Seattle, exiting at the Washington Park Arboretum exit. Follow arboretum signs onto East Lake Washington Boulevard to East Foster Island Road (left), toward Graham Visitor Center. Foster Island Road parking is on the left. The second parking lot is the easiest place from which to carry boats to the water.

More information: Seattle Parks Department, (206) 684-4075.
Graham Visitor Center, (206) 543-8800.

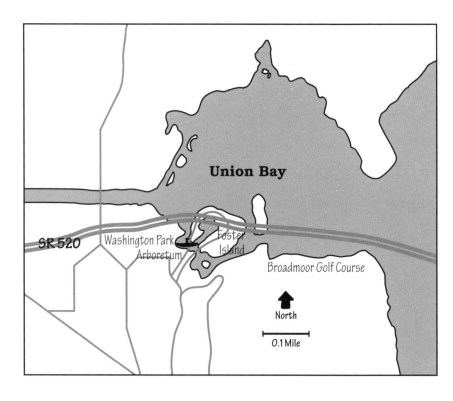

Rating: Beginner

This is truly an urban paddle, easily accessible from the Seattle metropolitan area. However, this also means there's a constant roar of traffic in the background. Still, if you ignore the road sounds, the area is a duck and goose haven and patches of pond lilies give it a feeling of getting away from it all.

My favorite way to paddle here is to put in at the park and paddle a short distance to the right, then go right under the footbridge. It is quieter here and the ducks seem to like it, too.

Even though you're in the city, you might want your binoculars and a camera for this paddling outing.

Other attractions: The trail system to Foster Island offers a nice walk; the visitor center and 200-acre arboretum are also worth a gander. They happily accept donations if you're impressed with the area.

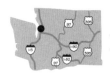

Lake Sammamish

Maps and charts: Seattle city map.

Access: Three access points discussed, though others possible. Launch at Lake Sammamish State Park at the southern end of the lake or up the eastside of the lake a short distance at the public launch (fee), or at Idylwood Park on the northwest bank.

Mileage: The lake is approximately 10 miles long.

Motors: No restrictions.

Directions: From US 90 East take Exit #15, directing you to Lake Sammamish State Park. The signs direct you left onto NW Sammamish then right into the park. Or, to launch at the public boat launch northeast of the state park, take the same exit off I-90 but go straight on NW Sammamish Road, then left on East Lake Sammamish Parkway SE, then left into the boat launch. Signs directing you to both places are well placed and easy to follow.

To launch at Idylwood Park on the northwest bank, take SR 520 east, instead of I-90. Stay on SR 520 until you reach SR 901, also named West Lake Sammamish Parkway NE, where you go right. Idylwood Park will be on the left.

More information: For possible paddling partners, or for more information, try the Seattle Sea Kayak Club, (425) 821-1021.
Tiger Mountain paragliding information, (425) 432-8900.

Rating: Beginner to expert

L ake Sammamish is large and exposed. It is also riddled with motorboats when-ever the weather is good. However, it is close to Seattle and there is plenty of water for everyone. Also, it makes for a perfect paddle on a cloudy or rainy day, which we do see a few of in the Northwest.

The state park on the south end of the lake has a nice beach for sand play and plenty of grass for frisbees, etc. This is also where Issaquah Creek comes in.

The public boat launch on the east side of the lake gets a lot of use, and I recom-mend avoiding it with kayaks and canoes unless you're there during the off-season.

Idylwood Park is nice, but exposed. Sammamish River comes in just north of the park and, like Issaquah Creek, could make for a nice side trip when water flows permit.

Other attractions: When I was at the park, a paragliding class was going on. Tons of fun, if you're ready to get out of the water and into the air.

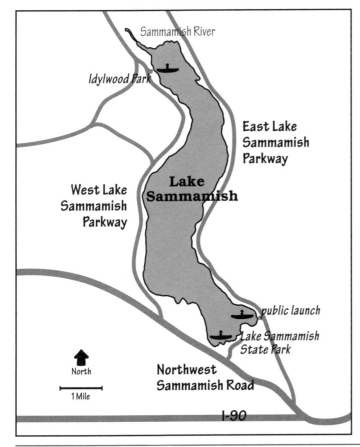

Cozy Cove/Yarrow Bay

Maps and charts: Seattle city map.

Access: Launch at the small public access put-in on 42nd Street NE.

Mileage: On Lake Washington in the city - paddle mileage virtually unlimited.

Motors: Launch site is not accessible to trailered boats.

Directions: From Seattle take SR 520 east. Take the first exit over the bridge and turn right onto 84th Avenue, then left on 24th and left again on 92nd Avenue NE. Take 92nd Avenue NE to 42nd Street NE, where you turn left and go to the end of the small residential street.

More information: Washington Water Trails Association, (206) 545-9161.

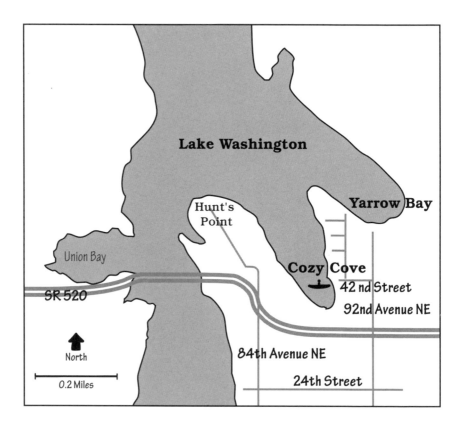

Rating: Beginner to expert

The biggest advantages to this urban paddle are that most maps don't show the small canoe and kayak launch, and motorboats can't launch here. The drawback is that you can't leave your vehicle right at the put-in and need to find a curbside parking spot nearby.

As for the paddle itself, in Cozy Cove you are between Hunt's Point and Yarrow Point, so you may get some protection from wind that might be whipping out in the middle of the lake.

There were geese all around the launch, but otherwise, don't expect much wildlife viewing here. What you can check out are homes and boats along Lake Washington.

However, if you paddle around Yarrow Point to the east, into Yarrow Bay, the south end of this bay is a marshy wetland area with no foot traffic or development allowed. If you paddle close to shore, you will likely see some waterfowl.

The launch nearby, just north of Yarrow Bay, is a large boat marina and not very suitable for small craft.

Other attractions: The short walking trails around Yarrow Bay are nice, but don't get you into the wetland. Still, it is a pleasant place for a morning or evening walk, to stretch your legs before or after a stint on the water. There are many other points on Lake Washington to see and Mercer Slough is a more private, nearby paddle. I don't cover it in this book because it is well described in others.

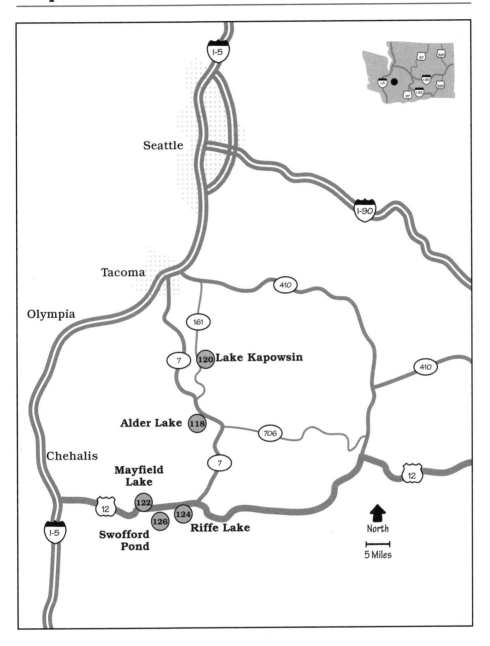

Alder Lake

Maps and charts: Washington state map, US Forest Service Gifford Pinchot National Forest map.

Access: Launch from any of three ramps on the lake. At Rocky Point boat launch about one third of the way up the lake, Sunny Beach Point Park about three quarters of the way up the lake, or at Alder Lake Park a short distance beyond Sunny Beach.

Mileage: Approximately 60 miles from Tacoma, 90 miles from Seattle, and 150 miles from Portland. Lake mileage: Approximately 15 miles long.

Motors: Virtually unrestricted except no-wake zones near shorelines and swimming facilities.

Directions: From Portland, take I-5 north to US 12 east. Go east on US 12 to SR 7 north to the lake.

From Tacoma or Seattle, take SR 7 from Tacoma south toward Rainier and the lake.

More information: Seattle Chamber of Commerce, (206) 389-7200.
Gifford Pinchot National Forest headquarters, (360) 891-5000.

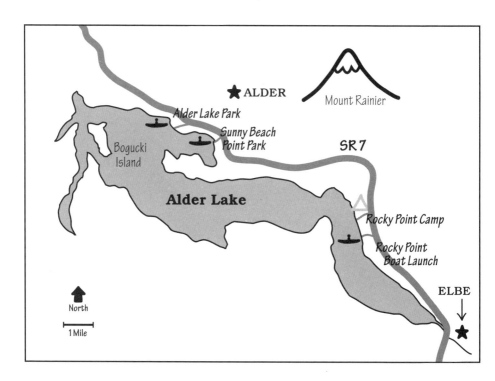

Rating: Intermediate to expert

When I pulled in to Rocky Point boat launch, 2 miles north of the town of Elbe, the wind was howling; but windsurfers and hawks, both soaring, encouraged me to check out the lake anyway.

Once up at Sunny Beach Point Park, the lake looked more inviting for paddlers, as I found the area protected with nice beach, swim and picnic areas. The walk to the water was a bit longer than from the small Rocky Point launch, but worth the walk for the quiet, more protected waterway.

Less than a mile up from Sunny Beach is Alder Lake Park, in the town of Alder. You can launch there, but I don't recommend it on a busy motorboater day, as this large launch is full on summer weekends. If you're in the area for more than a day trip, Alder Lake Park is a nice place to camp.

The lake has many arms and nooks to paddle up and explore (especially along the northeast and northwest shores), and the views of Rainier are unbeatable, though I'm a bit biased, since Rainier is one of my favorite Northwest mountains.

Other attractions: Eatonville is less than 10 miles north of the lake and hosts an Art Festival, usually held in mid-August.

Lake Kapowsin

Maps and charts: Washington state map.

Access: One launch at the north end of the lake. Small launch fee.

Mileage: 190 miles from Portland. 70 miles from Seattle. Less than 40 miles from Tacoma. Lake mileage: 3.5 miles long.

Motors: 5 mph

Directions: From Portland, take I-5 north to US 12. Go east on US 12 to SR 7 north then to SR 161 north. Take a right on Orville Road, which takes you around Ohop Lake and northward. Stay on Orville Road in Kapowsin, by turning right at the "T." Turn right into Erickson's boat rental lot and launch near the north end of the lake.

From Seattle or Tacoma, head south on SR 7 from Tacoma. Turn left onto Kapowsin Road or 304th Street E., and continue to the lake and single launch site at Erickson's.

More information: Eastern Pierce County Chamber of Commerce, (253) 845-6755.
Fairs information hotline, (253) 841-5045.
IP Pacific, for day use or any camping permit, (800) 782-1493.

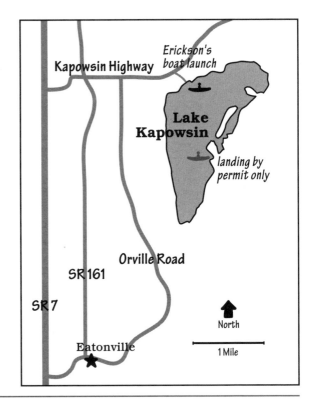

Rating: Beginner

Kapowsin's appeal is that motors are slowed to a crawl by speed regulations on the lake, eliminating jet skiers and speed boaters. There are also no homes around the lake, so it has a wilderness feel, especially if you cross the lake from the launch site and go behind the island, so that you are paddling between the island and the eastside of the lake. This area is for birders, with bird songs filling the air.

Circumnavigating the 7-mile perimeter of the lake, I noticed a stark difference coming around to the west bank. Apparently, the east end of the lake is owned by IP Pacific and the west end is not public land either. Don't plan on landing anywhere, unless you secure a permit from IP Pacific first. It is easy to paddle around the lake, however, without needing to land en route.

During the two hours I paddled, I saw osprey and eagle. I also got a glimpse of Mount Rainier's tip, when paddling up the northwest side of the lake.

Locals warn of cougar around the area.

Boat rentals, either motor or not, are available at the one launch site on the lake.

Other attractions: Puyallup isn't far to the north. Call the Eastern Pierce County Chamber for annual events, or the fairgrounds for a schedule of their events.
The area is known for rodeo.

Mayfield Lake

Maps and charts: Washington state map, US Forest Service Gifford Pinchot National Forest map.

Access: Access the lake either at Mayfield County Park on US 12, Lake Mayfield Resort at the southern end, or Ike Kinswa State Park on the northern end of the lake.

Mileage: 90-100 miles from Portland. Lake mileage: 13 miles long, 3/4 mile wide.

Motors: No-wake zones in coves and within 200 feet of shore. 8 mph in these areas.

Directions: I-5 north from Portland to Exit #68, where you get onto US 12, 80 miles from Portland. Stay on US 12 until you cross the bridge over the lake. Turn right on Winston Creek Road and follow signs to recreation area and Lake Mayfield Resort near where Winston Creek enters Mayfield Lake. Or, continue on US 12 to the Mayfield County Park half way up the lake. Or, follow signs, turning left off of US 12 and heading north and east to Ike Kinswa State Park on the Tilton River, before you reach the US 12 bridge across Mayfield Lake.

More information: Mayfield Lake County Park camping, write to: Mayfield Lake County Park, 180 Beach Road, Mossyrock , WA 98564
Lake Mayfield Marina and Resort, (360) 985-2357.
Mayfield Lake County Park, (360) 985-2367.
Ike Kinswa State Park, (360) 983-3402.
Tacoma Public Utilities (water levels information), (888) 502-8690.

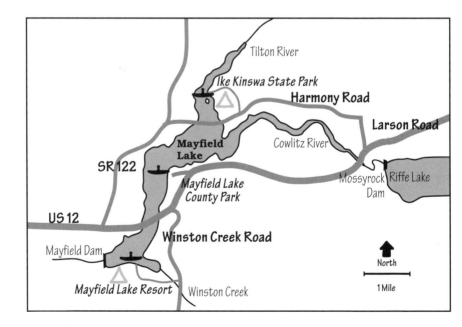

Rating: Beginner to expert

Mayfield Lake has more to offer than just a large lake to paddle. The resort near the southern end of the lake has adorable cabins overlooking the water named such things as the "Best Little Oar House." Tent camping is available on Lighthouse Island, which is a picturesque island with a lighthouse on it, and dock access to it.

One great thing about staying at Lake Mayfield Marina and Resort is easy access to the water. You can rent canoes or paddleboats there or leave your kayak or canoe tied to the dock so that you can come and go on the water without having to load and unload your boat off your vehicle every time you want to go for a paddle. Also, at the newly remodeled Lake Mayfield Resort, eagles nest and mate, giving quite a show in April and May.

There are three major coves on the lake. Winston Creek Cove, accessed via Lake Mayfield Marina and Resort; Tilton Creek Cove, at Ike Kinswa State Park; and Cowlitz River Cove. Upriver on both the Tilton and the Cowlitz rivers you can paddle, shouldered by steep rocky canyon walls. Here you stay clear of motorboats, which mostly stick to the lake.

Weekdays are quiet and wonderful on the lake, but summer weekends are crazy.

The fishing opportunities are plentiful, including fishing for the famous tiger musky, which was introduced as an ecological experiment to keep down squaw fish populations on the lake. This tiger musky is a sterile hybrid between muscaline and northern pike, and grows to over 36 inches before reaching legal keeper size. Also in the lake are three land-locked salmon species — coho, kokanee, and surprisingly, chinook, as well as several species of trout, catfish, bass and perch. Aside from fish and eagle, watch for coyote, beaver, and deer galore.

Other attractions: The tallest dam in Washington, Mossyrock Dam, is right up the road between Mayfield and Riffe lakes, and worth a look if you're interested in human-made wonders.

Riffe Lake

Maps and charts: Washington state map, US Forest Service Gifford Pinchot National Forest map.

Access: Four launches on the lake, including Mossyrock Park at the west end, Swofford Pond/Riffe Lake a bit further to the south beyond the park, Kosmos boat launch near the northeast end of the lake, and Taidnapam Park on the Cowlitz River at the eastern-most side of the lake.

Mileage: 115 miles from Portland. Lake mileage: Approximately 25 miles from dam to dam.

Motors: Lewis County ordinance states that motorboats must not produce damaging wake or motor in excess of 8 mph within 200 feet of any shore, dock, or public swimming area.

Directions: I-5 to Exit #68, (80 miles north of Portland) onto US 12 East. Drive Highway 12 for approximately 20 miles and turn right on Williams Street in the town of Mossyrock. Turn left onto State Street, which becomes Mossyrock Road, then Ajlune Road, which leads into Mossyrock Park. If launching at Swofford Pond/Riffe Lake area, turn right onto Swofford Road instead of continuing straight on Ajlune Road. Once at Swofford Pond, turn left and continue along the lake, until you pass Royal View Road on the left. Take the next left turn down a short unnamed dirt road with a sign warning against off-road vehicle use to a cove on Riffe Lake.

If launching at Kosmos Boat Launch or Taidnapam Park on the Cowlitz, continue on Highway 12 past Mossyrock Dam, to your clearly marked launch site.

More information: tacomapower.com website has reservation applications for camping at Taidnapam Park or Mossyrock Park on Riffe Lake, as well as maps of the area. To talk to a real person at: Taidnapam Park, (360) 497-7077.

Mossyrock Park, (360) 983-3900.

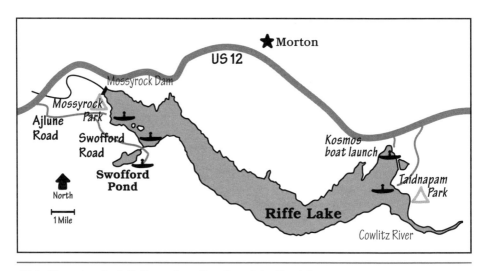

Rating: Expert (due to distance and exposure)

The four launches on Riffe Lake are quite different from one another. The one at Mossyrock Park, near Mossyrock Dam, is closest to I-5 and easy to find. If you're sick of driving and just want to jump out and paddle, it also has an enormous park for child's play and camping.

The Taidnapam Park launch gives you a place to launch with wind protection, since you can paddle up the Cowlitz River for about three miles, instead of into exposed Riffe Lake. You can camp there, too.

You can try Kosmos boat launch, where launching and camping are free on the northeast side of the lake before Taidnapam Park.

If the launches are crazy with motorboat traffic, try my secret put-in where Swofford Pond is on one side of the road and Riffe Lake is on the other. Here, you'll be able to launch quietly in a small cove on the southwest side of Riffe Lake. It's free, too.

Except near Taidnapam Park or other coves that are tucked away on Riffe, the lake has an ocean-like feel — enormous and exposed. Don't get caught in the strong late afternoon winds as you return to your launch site.

For strong paddlers who want a long workout paddle, or for those who like to cover some distance in a day, this 20-mile lake is for you.

According to the personnel at this Tacoma Power-run recreation facility, fishing at Swofford/Riffe junction is good. If you are looking for peace and quiet while fishing, try this area on the lake, or come in the off-season. The recreation area is open year round.

Other attractions: Mossyrock Dam is responsible for creating Riffe lake, and is the tallest dam in Washington, so it's worth a look if you're into human-made wonders.

Swofford Pond

Maps and charts: Washington state map.

Access: Pullouts along the road around the small lake.

Mileage: Approximately 115 miles from Portland. Lake mileage: 1.5 miles long.

Motors: No combustible motors allowed.

Directions: Approximately 4.5 miles east of Mossyrock, I-5 to Exit #68, (80 miles north of Portland) onto US 12 East. Drive Highway 12 for approximately 20 miles and turn right on Williams Street in the town of Mossyrock. Turn left onto State Street, which becomes Mossyrock Road, then Ajlune Road, leading into Mossyrock Park. Turn right onto Swofford Road instead of continuing straight on Ajlune Road into the park. Once at Swofford Pond, turn left at the split and find a pullout to launch.

More information: Camping reservations at Mossyrock Park are by application only. For an application, call: (360) 983-3900. Reservations must be made two weeks prior to arrival.

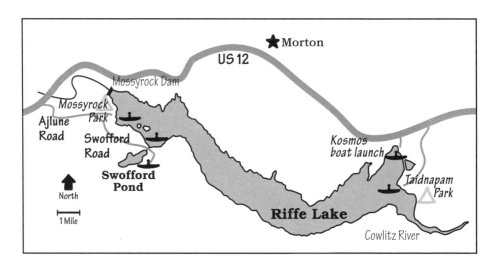

Rating: Beginner

Swofford Pond is larger than its name implies and is a birder's dream at dawn and dusk. The wood ducks are beautiful and plentiful. On land, watch for deer and elk.

The marshy area of the lake is accessible by boardwalk over the wetland. Stay on the boardwalk trail in this delicate wildlife area.

This lake won't keep you busy paddling all day, so plan to fish and float, or picnic on this quiet hideaway lake and swap stories with fishermen.

You can also head over to Riffe Lake for larger environs and a more open feel.

Other attractions: Mossyrock Dam goes 325 feet down to the water, making it Washington's tallest dam. It anchors another 240 feet below the ground into bedrock. If you're interested in observing monumental human engineering and workmanship, this dam is worth a visit.

Mossyrock Park is enormous, and is complete with beaches, swimming areas, swing sets, and overnight camping.

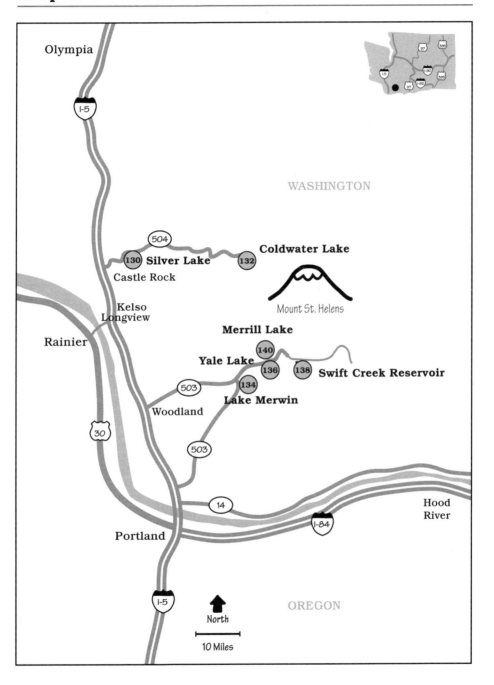

Silver Lake

Maps and charts: US Forest Service Gifford Pinchot National Forest map, Washington state map, Mount St. Helens National Volcanic Monument map.

Access: There are three launches on the lake. Two are private facilities that allow you to park and launch for a small fee. The third is for public access, but you'll need an Access Stewardship Decal on your vehicle. All three launches have advantages, though my favorite is at the Silver Lake Motel and Resort because it is near the largest no-wake area on the lake.

Mileage: 65 miles from Portland. 100 miles from Seattle. Lake mileage: 4 1/2 miles long and 2 miles across.

Motors: Several no-wake zone pockets on the lake.

Directions: Take I-5 to SR 504 East, Exit #49, near Castle Rock. Take SR 504 approximately 6 miles to Silver Lake Motel and Resort just beyond Seaquest State Park.

Alternate Launch: Continue on SR 504 east beyond the Silver Lake Motel and Resort, turning right on Kerr Road just before milepost 8. This takes you down to the public access launch on the north end of the lake.

Alternate launch: Head east on SR 504 to Hall Road. Take a right onto Hall, then right again on Streeter Road to the Streeter Resort on the east end of the lake.

More information: Silver Lake Motel and Resort, (360) 274-6141.
Streeters Resort, (360) 274-6112.
Washington State Park reservations, (800) 452-5687.
Washington State Park information, (800) 233-0321.
Coldwater Ridge Visitor Center, (360) 274-2131.

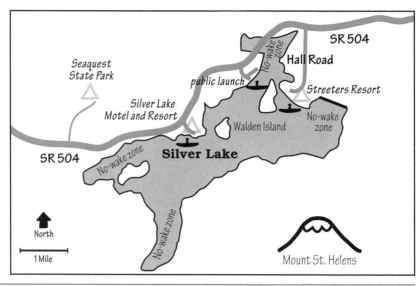

Rating: Beginner to expert

Silver Lake was a pleasant surprise. The lake is large and the view of Mount St. Helens in the distance is impressive. The nicest surprise, however, was finding out that there are large no-wake zone sections on the lake, which are strictly enforced.

Launching from the Silver Lake Resort and going west, you get into some beautiful marshes with an abundance of pond lilies.Going east from the resort, takes you out into the open waters where jet skiers sometimes race around. I avoid this hair-raising section of the lake, except to cross into the next no-wake zone.

The paddle around Walden Island is unique, with grasses creating a channel along one side of the island, leaving only a canal to access houses on that side. The island is private property, but it is worth paddling around to view the houses built entirely from materials boated in.

The launches further up the lake give easier access to the top two no-wake zones, but the areas are shallow. My favorite area of the lake is the southwest end because there is the most no-wake zone paddling there.

Eagles mate over the lake, I'm told, and the area is known for its bass fishing. You'll also find bluegill, crappie, perch, catfish, and trout.

Boats and canoes are available for rent at the resorts and at a drive-up dock halfway up the lake.

If you're in the area for more than a day's paddle, camping is available at the resorts, though this is not a wilderness experience. The Seaquest State Park is more forested, but is across SR 504 from the lake.

Other attractions: You aren't far from the Mount St. Helens visitors centers, which are always worth a visit. Also, Silver Lake Motel and Resort rents rooms overlooking the lake, where you can actually fish from your balcony. There are plenty of hiking trails in the area, too.

Coldwater Lake

Maps and charts: Mount St. Helens National Volcanic Monument map, Washington state map, US Forest Service Gifford Pinchot National Forest map.

Access: Only one launch on the lake, at the southern end.

Mileage: 100 miles from Portland. 150 miles from Seattle. Lake mileage: 4 miles long.

Motors: Electric motors only.

Directions: Take I-5 to Exit #49 near Castle Rock onto SR 504. Go east for approximately 40 miles, following signs to Coldwater Ridge Visitor Center. Follow the signs directing you 2 miles below the visitor center to the lake. You may want to stop at the visitor center first, to buy your required monument passes for the day.

More information: Hoffstadt Bluffs information and reservations, (800) 752-VIEW. Coldwater Ridge Visitor Center, (360) 274-2131.

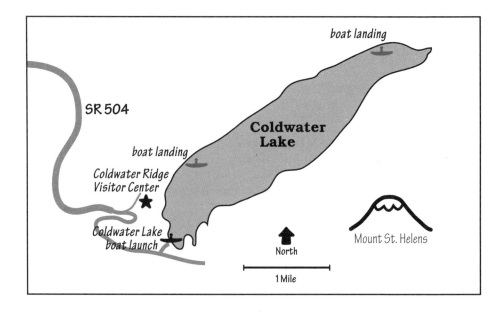

Rating: Beginner to intermediate

If I were naming writer's choice awards to special lakes, this one would be high on the list. This 766-acre lake represents solitude at its finest.

Many maps still don't show a boat ramp on Coldwater Lake. This inaccuracy, and the motor restrictions, keep most boaters away.

The boardwalk at the south end of the lake is popular with tourists and hikers, but when you launch and paddle away, you are usually alone on the water.

You see Mount St. Helens looming in one direction and its devastation as you paddle northeastward. The views are unique to the northwest and an awesome reminder of the region's wild power.

Landing is not allowed around the lake, even though there are many spots. The only areas you can tread on land, beyond the hiking trail, are boat landings at mile 1 and mile 4 along the lake. The clearly marked landings are both on the left as you paddle up the lake.

Wind warnings posted at the launch site tell the story of high, gusty winds on a shallow lake, but when I was there, the winds were quite manageable with a kayak and the 8-mile round trip paddle was utterly relaxing.

I'm not a birder, but I did recognize ouzel, kingfisher and, I'm almost certain, widgeon.

Fishing is permitted and the lake is stocked with rainbow trout.

The brushy growth on the lake perimeter, including wildflowers still blooming in mid-August, keep the area from seeming too stark after the eruption's destruction.

What struck me more than anything was the sacred quiet of the area. The only noises I heard were birds chattering occasionally and water spilling into the lake from small mountain runoff streams.

Other attractions: Coldwater Ridge Visitor Center is always worth the stop, no matter how many times you've been there. Hoffstadt Bluffs Visitor Center and others offer helicopter tours if you want to see the area from the air.

Lake Merwin

Maps and charts: US Forest Service Mount St. Helens National Volcanic Monument map, US Forest Service Gifford Pinchot National Forest map, Washington state map.

Access: Speelyai Bay Recreation Area on the east end of the lake. Park fee, but no launch fee unless boats are on trailers. Alternate launch site at Cresap Bay near Yale Dam.

Mileage: From Portland, 50 miles to the launch site on the east end of the Lake. Lake mileage: Approximately 10 miles long.

Motors: 40 mph speed limit on the lake. No wake in bays and recreation areas, 5 mph within 200 feet of shore.

Directions: Take I-5 north from Portland to the Woodland Exit #21, onto SR 503 heading east. Speelyai Bay Recreation Area gates are clearly marked on the right. To launch at Cresap Bay, continue on SR 503 to SR 503 South. Go right toward Battleground on SR 503S to Frasier Road. Left on Frasier toward Saddle Dam, Yale Lake. Where the road forks, go right to Cresap Bay. Left takes you to the other side of the dam to Yale Lake.

More information: No camping at Speelyai, but camping at Cresap Bay, (503) 813-6666 for reservations.
Northwest Forest Pass or monument pass information, (800) 270-7504. Passes sold at all National Forest offices and many retail outlets.

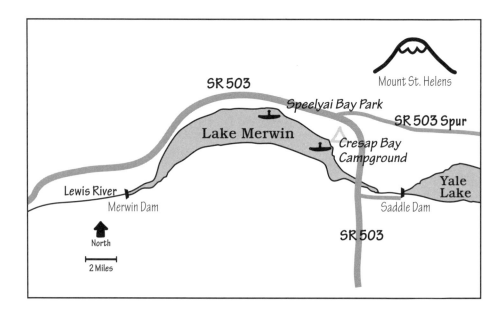

Rating: Beginner to expert

I didn't always think of Mount St. Helens as a Portland metropolitan area paddle, but why not? With only an hour drive to reach the water on the south side of St. Helens, the reservoir recreation sites provide easy access to the water, where you'll have some great mountain views and plenty of room to let it rip. The area is perfect if paddling a long way as a training workout appeals to you.

Wind funnels down the chain of lakes — Merwin, Yale, and Swift, sometimes, but the bays, such as Speelyai and Cresap, offer protection, as does the shoreline. The paddle from one bay to the other, Speelyai to Cresap (approximately 5 miles one way), is a good day paddle. Because of reservoir elevation changes, I will not mention landings, other than to say there were plenty of possible beaches the day I was there.

The only problem with the area is that it does get crowded at the boat launches, as there are few of them on the large, narrow lake. An easy fix is to launch along the beach with your canoe or kayak, avoiding competition for ramp time with the motorists. When I was at Speelyai Bay, there was a perfect launch beach at the end of the parking lot, behind an enormous stump at the turnaround, though with fluctuating water levels the beach may be under water when you arrive. The point is, as a paddler who doesn't need a constructed boat launch, avoid them when you can, cutting down on launch stress.

As for the camping at the lake, the campsites are a short distance away from the water. It isn't possible to leave boats afloat during your camping experience. Also, the campgrounds are popular and usually fill up by Friday afternoons during midsummer.

Other attractions: At the end of the Speelyai Bay parking lot, there is also a trail leading out to the point of Speelyai Bay. The grassy picnic area grounds are lovely, but for a more private picnic, try the short hike out to the point.

You're in volcano country. If you haven't been already, check out Ape Caves for a cool underground hike. Continue on SR 503 Spur eastward to Ape Caves turnoff. For this side trip, bring sweaters and long pants, even on the hottest day of the year. Also, you'll need a Northwest Forest Pass, which is not needed at the Pacific Power recreation sites, Speelyai Bay, or Cresap Bay.

Yale Lake

Maps and charts: US Forest Service Mount St. Helens National Volcanic Monument map, US Forest Service Gifford Pinchot National Forest map, Washington state map.

Access: Four launches on Yale Lake. All easily accessible on SR 503 Spur east except Saddle Dam launch which is off SR 503 South.

Mileage: 60 miles from Portland. Lake mileage: Over 12 miles.

Motors: 40 mph speed limit. No-wake in recreation areas, 5 mph within 200 feet of shore.

Directions: Take I-5 to Woodland, Exit #21 to SR 503. Go on SR 503 heading east to either SR 503 South (for Saddle Dam launch) or SR 503 Spur east for all other Yale Lake access. For Saddle Dam, take SR 503 South junction to the right at Jack's Restaurant and Store. Turn left onto Frasier Road and follow signs to the dam and recreation area.

More information: Camping first come, first served, except at Cougar Park. Cougar Park tent camping, (360) 813-6666.

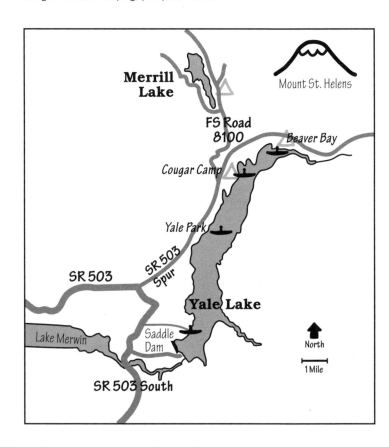

Rating: Beginner to expert

Yale Lake has glorious views of Mount St. Helens. Though the wind whips down the narrow lake at times, there are plenty of places to hide.

If you launch at Saddle Dam, you can paddle to Siouxon Creek a couple miles up and turn into the arm, a short distance up the creek. This can be a nice, quiet paddle. The area has a boat launch, beach, and dock, so you can choose your launch position according to how heavily used the ramps are that day. No sense stressing over motorboaters, when you can quietly put in out of their way.

Yale Park, Cougar Park, and Beaver Bay are similar recreation sites, all operated by the local power company. The parks are nice for picnicking, have roped off swimming areas, and are well-maintained. Entrance fees are required in all parks, though there is no charge to launch kayaks and canoes (anything without a trailer).

The long exposed lake gets plenty of waterskier and jet skier traffic, but the lake is enormous, so there's plenty of room for everyone.

My favorite launch site is Beaver Bay because of the wind protection there and because of the island in the bay. This launch seems smaller and quieter than the others, and the area feels more like a paddler's haunt. If you paddle up the bay toward the power lines and dam, do so with care, as the water starts to move more swiftly there.

On summer afternoons, there are often whitecaps down the center of the lake, so stay close to shore unless you are practicing your bracing, surfing or rescue skills. Even then, be cautious of motorboaters speeding by, remembering that you are often difficult to see on the water, especially by speeders that aren't on the lookout.

Eagles and osprey frequent the area, as do deer and other wildlife.

Other attractions: If you're near Yale or Merwin lakes you ought to know that, "everyone meets at Jack's," according to the general store's owner, Michael Livingston, at Junction SR 503 South and SR 503 Spur. You can get a bite to eat or pick up any forgotten essentials there.

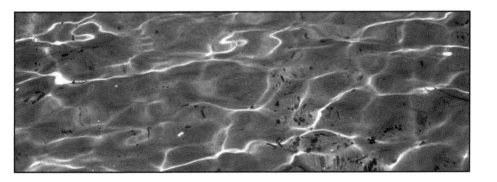

Swift Creek Reservoir

Maps and charts: US Forest Service Mount St. Helens National Volcanic Monument map, US Forest Service Gifford Pinchot National Forest map, Washington state map.

Access: One launch at the north end of the lake.

Mileage: Approximately 75 miles northeast of Portland. Lake mileage: Approximately 12 miles long.

Motors: 40 mph speed limit. No wake in recreation areas, 5 mph within 200 feet of shore.

Directions: Take I-5 to Woodland Exit #21 to SR 503. Go east on SR 503 to either SR 503 South (for Saddle Dam launch) or SR 503 Spur east to Swift Forest Camp.

More information: Gifford Pinchot National Forest Service headquarters, (360) 891-5000.

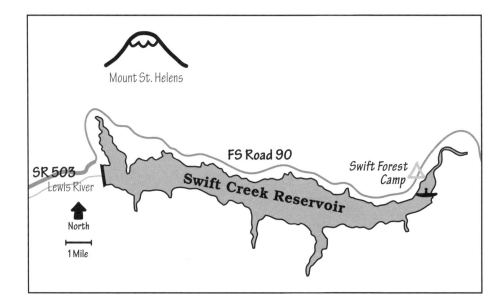

Rating: Intermediate to expert

Floating logs keep most boaters out of Swift Reservoir, according to forest service personnel at nearby Ape Caves. This makes for a nice kayaking opportunity in the right conditions. However, this area tops a chain of dammed lakes in a valley and the wind funnels and whips the water on the reservoir often.

This elongated lake is great for kayak race trainers who want to get in a long, straight paddle.

Landings when I was there were slim, but there are more at lower water levels. The south end of the lake is difficult to access and makes for a long day's paddle from the north launch, but it is inspiring and has great views of Mount St. Helens.

The campground at the north end of the lake is popular and often full on summer weekends. Come early or come prepared to move on after a day's paddle.

Other attractions: Nearby Ape Caves is worth the hike through if you have time. If you do the entire hike, be sure you have help with small children, as there are some boulder climbs and scrambles in the dark. And it really is dark. Bring a lantern, or rent one at the entrance.

Mount St. Helens Monument passes are required and can be purchased at the cave entrance as well.

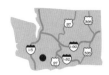

Merrill Lake

Maps and charts: US Forest Service Mount St. Helens National Volcanic Monument map, US Forest Service Gifford Pinchot National Forest map, Washington state map.

Access: Merrill Lake Campground and boat ramp.

Mileage: 70 miles from Portland. Lake mileage: Approximately 2 miles long.

Motors: 5 mph.

Directions: Take I-5 to Woodland Exit #21 onto SR 503, then SR 503 east to milepost 35 just past Yale Park. Turn left onto Forest Service Road #8100. Turn left at sign leading to Kalama Horse Camp, then left again into Merrill Lake Campground.

More information: Washington Department of Natural Resources SW region, (800) 527-3305.

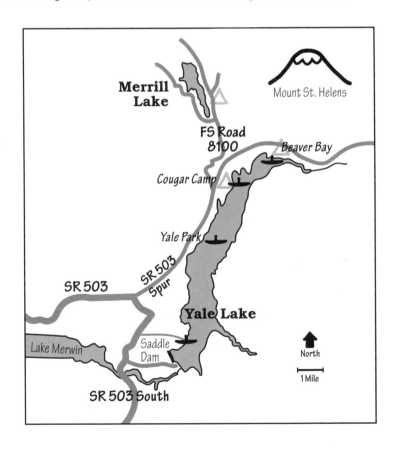

Rating: Beginner

If you're looking for quiet on the water near Mount St. Helens, here's your lake.

But, if you want to motor, don't fish, and if you want to fish, don't motor. Such are the rules at Merrill Lake. Also, Department of Natural Resources personnel ask that you only camp in the tent-only campground, not across the lake, as you'll see others do.

As for the paddling, the lake has nooks and crannies that make it feel larger than its 2-mile length. The shallow depth makes the area good for practicing wet exits and re-entries. Even if you want to paddle larger waters, the drive up to the lake is worthwhile for the panoramic views of Yale Lake below.

The fishing is supposed to be superb, according to a fly-fisherman I spoke to at the lake. But leave your bait at home. This lake is fly-fishing only, and only from the shore or from a boat without a motor.

Here's something that's getting more rare all the time: No fees on Merrill Lake.

Other attractions: Meet at Jack's General Store and Restaurant at the SR 503 South and SR 503 Spur Junction if you need a rendezvous spot for a group. Check out the Ape Caves underground hiking to cool your day down a bit, or drive to one of the Mount St. Helens Visitor Centers if you've never been.

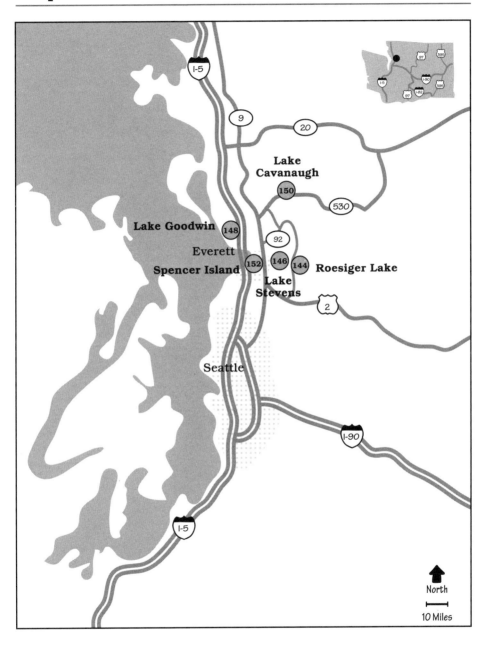

Roesiger Lake

Maps and charts: Washington state map, Mount Baker-Snoqualmie National Forest map.

Access: US Fish and Wildlife public launch on the south end of the lake (Access Stewardship Decal required and available where hunting and fishing licenses are sold), and the county park one mile farther up the east side of the lake.

Mileage: Approximately 40 miles from Seattle and 15 miles from Everett. Lake mileage: Approximately 3+ miles long.

Motors: 8 mph in the stem between north and south ends of the lake. 35 mph in water-skiing course areas of the lake and 8 mph before 10:30 a.m. and after 5:30 p.m.

Waterskiing May 25 - Sept. 25 only. Skiing counterclockwise.

Directions: Take SR 9 to 20th Street (Hewitt), and go right. Hewitt turns to Williams then to Machias Cutoff. Turn right, then right again onto S. Machias Road, then left onto Dubuque Road just beyond Centennial School. Go left on South Roesiger Lake Road, right at the "Y," left on Middle Shore Road and left to the public launch parking.

More Information: Group Campground Reservations, (360) 568-2274. Snohomish County Tourism Bureau, (888) 338-0976.

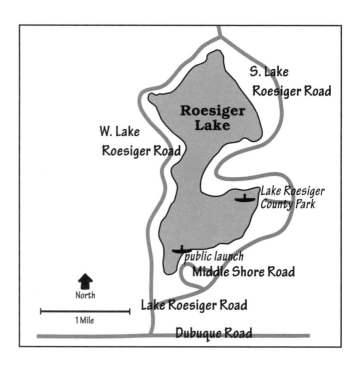

Rating: Beginner to intermediate

Roesiger Lake is a bit off the beaten path, but is popular with waterskiers in midsummer nonetheless.

Still, waterskiing season on the lake is only four months long, so paddlers can take full advantage of the lake at its quietest the other five months of the year.

The best part of the lake to paddle may be the middle lake where the 8 mph restriction applies even during ski season. To access this area best, launch at the county park up the east side of the lake.

If you want to round up a group, there is a group campground across from the county park.

This long lake, with views of glaciers south and east, is a nice getaway paddle, though much of the area is privately owned.

It is generally a quieter paddle than nearby Lake Stevens.

Other attractions: Snohomish is nearby to the west, and the town of Monroe is just to the south. Both are active in the arts and tourism. Call the Snohomish County Tourism Bureau to see what is happening when you're planning to be in the area. This is pumpkin patch/hay maze country, with different farms offering different displays and activities, such as hay rides, and the Peter Rabbit Story Trail at The Farm in Snohomish.

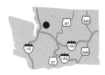

Lake Stevens

Maps and charts: East Snohomish and surrounding communities street map (available from Chamber of Commerce), Washington state map, US Forest Service Mount Baker-Snoqualmie National Forest map.

Access: Two launches. One at Lundeen Park on the north shore, and the other at Wyatt Park at the southwest end of the lake. Fee at Wyatt Park.

Mileage: 30 miles from Seattle. Lake mileage: Approximately 8 mile perimeter. 1,040- acre lake.

Motors: 35 mph speed limit. Counterclockwise boating when over 8 mph.

Directions: Take I-5 north to Exit #194, 25 miles north of Seattle onto US 2 heading east. Approximately one mile to Lake Stevens, exit onto SR 204 heading east. From SR 204, go left onto SR 9 going north. Half-mile up SR 9, go right onto Lundeen Parkway, then right into Lundeen Park. For Wyatt Park launch, stay on SR 204 (instead of turning onto SR 9) through the traffic light, as if you're going into the Safeway parking lot. Take a sharp left onto the frontage road, then right onto Davies Road. Follow Davies Road around to the right on the west side of the lake to Wyatt County Park. There will likely be an easier way into Wyatt Park most of the time, but road construction made access difficult when I visited.

More information: Lake Stevens Chamber of Commerce, (206) 334-0433.

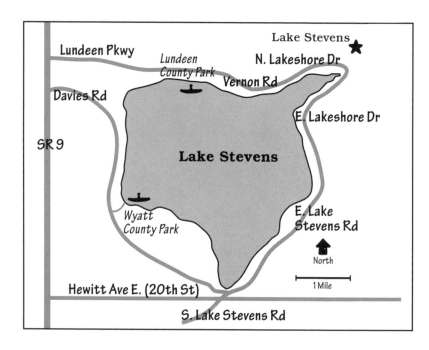

Rating: Beginner

Lake Stevens has gorgeous views of Mount Baker looming in the distance to the north and views of the North Cascades to the east. It is the largest recreational lake in Snohomish County, and extremely popular in the summer. However, on a fall morning, the lake is quiet and perfect for a paddle.

You'll likely see eagle in the spring and if fishing, you may catch bass, trout, or kokanee.

The lake water has had its problems and health signs warn of swimmer's itch.

Launching from the grass at Lundeen Park is probably best when the lake is crowded, so that you're not competing for ramp space with motorboats.

Aside from the two park launches, there is supposedly access to the water in the town of Lake Stevens itself, near the city park, but I couldn't find it.

Other attractions: Locals tell me that the late July Aquafest is the most exciting annual event in the Lake Stevens area. Included are skiing races and exhibitions, a parade, arts and crafts, music, fireworks, and more.

Lake Goodwin

Maps and charts: Washington state map.

Access: Wenberg State Park on the southeast side of the lake (fee).

Mileage: Approximately 40 miles from Seattle. Lake mileage: 2+ miles long.

Motors: 35 mph. Travel counterclockwise when over 8 mph.

Directions: Take I-5 north to Smokey Point Exit (SR 531) near Marysville, north of Everett. Follow signs directing you to the state park, west of the freeway.

More information: Snohomish County Parks, (425) 388-6600.
Wenberg State Park camping reservations (Reservations Northwest), (800) 452-5687.

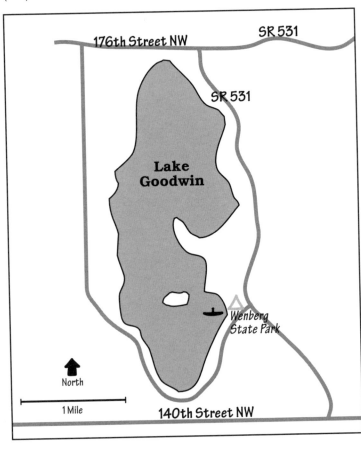

Rating: Beginner

L ike many of the lakes in the area, this shoreline is developed, making it a "home tour" paddle rather than a wilderness experience. Still, it is close to Seattle, Everett and Marysville, making the lake a good choice for a quick afternoon workout on the water if you live near any of these urban areas.

There are private campgrounds on the lake. Otherwise, your camping option is Wenberg State Park, which is expansive and well cared for. The drawback for campers, however, is that campsites don't have water frontage, making it impossible to launch your boat from camp.

The counterclockwise boat travel rule indicates that this lake is well traveled in summer. The best time to paddle here is midday, midweek, or during late fall and winter. The place was deserted in early October.

Enjoy looking for hovering and fishing eagle and osprey.

Other attractions: The Portage Wildlife Sanctuary is nearby and can give you the wilderness experience that the lake lacks. To get there, take the Smokey Point Exit, but go east to 67th Avenue NE, then left (north) for two miles to 204th Street, which is also called Cemetery Road. Take a left onto 204th Street. Portage Creek is on the right. Once at the sanctuary, enjoy the 157-acre wildlife reserve, walking along the trails that cross the wetland. You might see deer, hawk, raccoon, mink, beaver and, of course, plenty of waterfowl.

Lake Cavanaugh

Maps and charts: Washington state map, Skagit county map, US Forest Service Mount Baker-Snoqualmie National Forest map.

Access: One launch at the southwest end of the lake. Access Stewardship Decal required.

Mileage: Approximately 55 miles north of Seattle. Lake mileage: Approximately 4 miles long.

Motors: No-wake zone 150 feet from shoreline and after dusk. Skiing counterclockwise.

Directions: Heading north on I-5 from Seattle or Everett, take SR 530 (Exit #208) approximately 15 miles, to Lake Cavanaugh Road. Turn left on Lake Cavanaugh Road and continue for another 5 miles, to the lake. Turn left when you reach the lake (even though many maps indicate a right here) and the public launch is on the right.

More information: US Department of Natural Resources, (360) 856-3500.

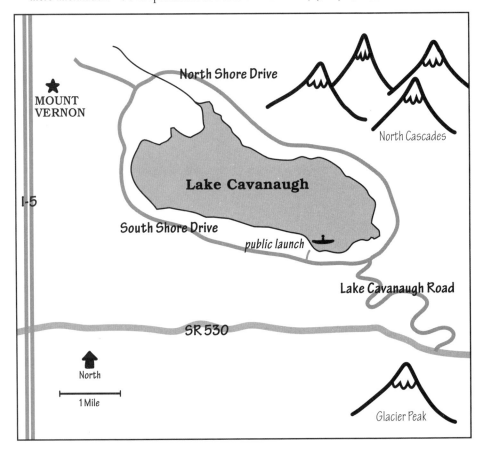

Rating: Beginner to intermediate

To save you a driving trip around the lake, I'll reiterate that maps indicate a right at the fork at the end of Lake Cavanaugh Road, then left into the public access launch, when, in fact, you need to turn left at the lake, then right into the public launch.

There is some logging around the lake in spots, and the shoreline is mostly private land; but, if you launch at the public launch and paddle northwest, you get some great views of the peaks southeast of the lake.

If you paddle all the way up the lake, you'll find some small islands to paddle around, near the west end.

I had a great sunset paddle on Lake Cavanaugh, quiet and still in early October. If you live nearby, it is worth the drive and you'll be rewarded with a good workout and mountain views as you paddle back to the launch, heading southeast.

Other attractions: Glacier Peak Wilderness is not far to the east and has excellent hiking.

Spencer Island

Maps and charts: Snohomish River Estuary Recreation Guide, Everett city map, Washington state map.

Access: Langus Riverfront Park on the Snohomish River or from the North in Marysville at Ebey Slough Boat Launch.

Mileage: 20 miles north of Seattle. Spencer Island circumnavigation from Langus Park, approximately 7 miles. Spencer Island acreage, 412-plus acres.

Motors: Shallow water at low tide along the west side of Spencer Island, on Union Slough, discourages most motorboaters, though motor traffic on the Snohomish River at the park put-in is often heavy and virtually unrestricted.

Directions: Take I-5 north to the Port of Everett, Exit #195. Go north on Marine View Drive, then north on SR 529, which heads into Maryville. Take the Marine Park exit onto 28th Place NE, then follow signs to Langus Riverfront Park. This will take you right on 35th Avenue, then left onto Ross Avenue. The public launch is on the right. Fee for trailered boats only.

To Ebey Slough in Marysville, take the Marysville exit off I-5 to 4th Avenue, then take a right on Beach Street. Turn right on 1st Street to the primitive launch under I-5 next to a lumber mill.

Note: Getting to either launch can be confusing. The Snohomish River Estuary Recreation Guide will help immensely in directing you to the launch as well as in guiding you on the water. The guide is available through Snohomish Parks and Recreation.

More information: Everett Chamber of Commerce, (425) 438-1487.
Snohomish County Parks and Recreation, (425) 339-1208.
Everett Center for the Arts, (425) 257-8380.

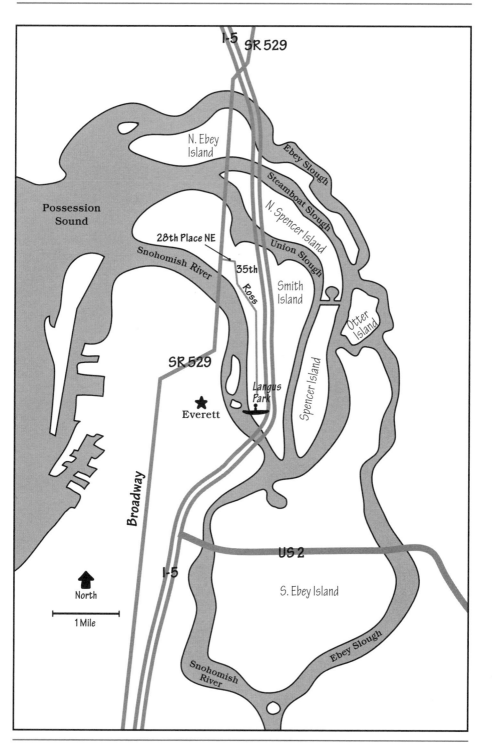

Spencer Island

This area is a well-kept secret, but I was lucky enough to get a guided tour by Charles Brennick, the author of the Snohomish River Estuary Guide. He works hard to promote this area as a paddling waterway, and once you've been there, I bet you'll be back for more.

This is the trip with the most wilderness feel of all the paddling excursions listed in this book, from Seattle northward.

Launching on the Snohomish River can be unnerving when there are motorboaters around, and if Langus Park is busy, I recommend driving past the park and using the pullout down the road by the bridge. Also, don't be discouraged by the roar of the freeway when you launch. Once in the sloughs around Spencer Island, you'll feel miles from all the traffic.

When you put in, head south on the Snohomish River, then take a left into the Steamboat Slough. At low tide, you can't circumnavigate Spencer Island, because you'll hit bottom in Union Slough. But when water levels allow, go left into Union Slough, paddling north, with Spencer Island on your right, until you get to Busey Cut, which separates Spencer Island from North Spencer. At Busey Cut, go right, paddle through the cut to Steamboat Slough, then head south down the east side of Spencer Island. Or gander farther north up Steamboat Slough toward Marysville. Paddling north on Steamboat Slough, beyond the cut, Otter Island will be on your right, North Spencer on your left.

Otter Island is Snohomish County property, saved from development or logging because the entire 164-acre island is a marshy swamp, according to Brennick. Try a side trip around Otter Island, which is flanked by Ebey Slough to the east and Steamboat Slough to the west. While you are welcome to paddle around Otter

Island, landing on the island is prohibited, as this is a wetland preservation area where bald eagle, red-tail hawk, and osprey nest.

Landing on Spencer is okay, and there is a hiking trail around its perimeter if you want to explore parts of the island from land. The northern half of South Spencer Island is Washington Department of Fish and Wildlife land where hunting is seasonally permitted. You may want to avoid the island altogether during the fall hunting season, or at least stay along the southern half.

There is talk of putting a small launch for non-motorized craft on Spencer Island's western shore. This would allow paddlers to avoid the busy Langus Park launch on the Snohomish River and shorten the paddling distance around Spencer Island. If you are in favor of such a launch site, call the Snohomish County Parks and Recreation office to let them know you'd use it.

During my paddle around the island, I saw harbor seal, otter, heron, geese, merganser, and kingfisher. Woodpecker, great horned owl, hawk, and coot, are just a few of the other bird species you're likely to see on the island.

Other attractions: Everett is not just a Seattle bedroom community. It has theaters, museums, restaurants, hotels, and festivals all its own.

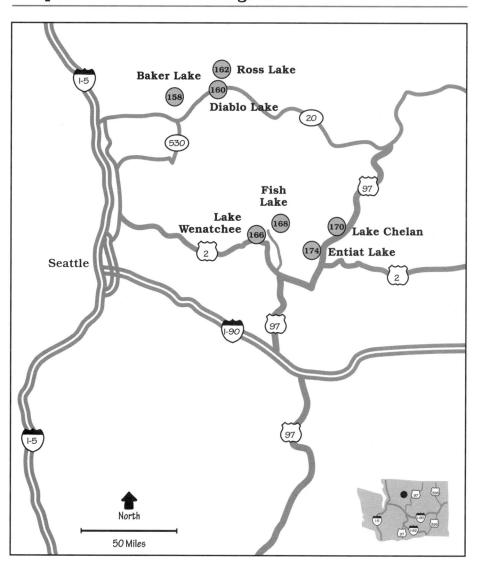

Baker Lake

Maps and Charts: US National Forest Service Mount Baker-Snoqualmie National Forest map, Green Trails topographic series, Lake Shannon, WA #46.

Access: Five boat ramp sites on the west side of the lake off Baker Lake Road.

Mileage: Approximately 100 miles east of Seattle. Lake mileage: 20 miles long.

Motors: Virtually unrestricted.

Directions: Take SR 20 east to Baker Lake Road just past milepost 82, west of Concrete. Turn left (north) onto Baker Lake Road and follow it to the lake.

More information: Concrete Chamber of Commerce, (360) 853-7042.
Sedro-Wooley Ranger District, (360) 856-5700.
Eagle Festival and Float trip, (360) 853-7009.
Camping at Baker Lake, (877) 444-6777.

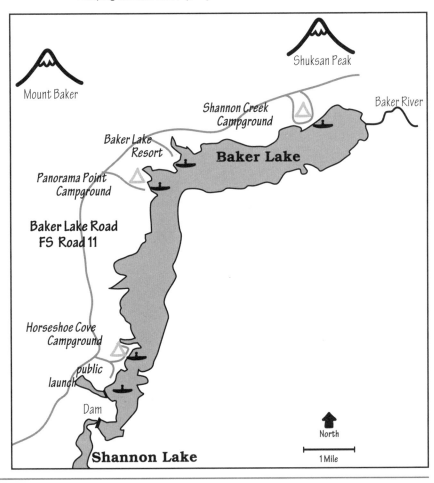

Rating: Beginner to expert

No better views of Mount Baker and Shuksan Peak exist than those you get from the water on Baker Lake. That, and the easy access from Seattle, explains why the lake is popular with paddlers and power boaters alike.

In mid-July, during the thirty minutes that I was at the Horseshoe Cove launch, over 30 vessels launched. All five campgrounds near the lake were full, as well.

Once on the water, the lake seems big enough for everyone, though I still recommend paddling the coves or close to shore to avoid collisions or high winds.

Panorama Point and Shannon Creek on the north end of the lake are both recommended put-ins on calm days because views from there are fantastic and you can make it to the northeast end of the lake and paddle the Baker River Inlet from these points.

As for making this a destination paddle, there is access to the water at Horseshoe Cove, Panorama Point, and Shannon Creek campgrounds, though not from the campsites themselves. This meant loading and unloading boats from our vehicles or carrying them from camp to the launch every time we wanted to paddle.

Park Creek and Boulder Creek campgrounds are on Boulder and Park Creeks, not right on Baker Lake. Because the campgrounds get crowded and you can't put your boat in the water from camp, if you live in Seattle, or nearby to the north or

east, I recommend Baker Lake more as a day trip than a destination area. You can make it in here for an afternoon expedition and still be home by dark.

Impressive is an understatement when describing sunset over the lake, and it's worth the evening jaunt out of the city, with or without a boat.

Deer and bear are in the area, as well as eagle and osprey, though eagles are more common along the Skagit River.

Other attractions: Baker Lake is 13 miles north of the town of Concrete, where the Baker and Skagit Rivers meet. Whitewater rafting the Skagit River and biking the Cascade Loop are popular.

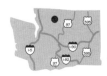

Diablo Lake

Maps and charts: Green Trails topographic series, Diablo Dam, WA #48, Washington state map, North Cascades National Park map.

Access: Launch at Colonial Creek Campground on Thunder Arm. Fee.

Mileage: 150 miles from Seattle. Lake mileage: 4.5 miles long , 2 miles up Thunder Arm.

Motors: Shallow on Thunder Arm at times. Few high-speed motors, mainly trolling motors.

Directions: Take SR 20 east, past Diablo Dam, to Colonial Creek after milepost 130. Turn right into the campground.

More information: Ross Deluxe Meal Tour or other tours by Seattle City Light, (206) 684-3030.
Colonial Creek Campground: first come, first served.
North Cascades National Park Ranger Station (boat-in camping permits), (360) 873-4500 Ext. 39.
Mount Baker-Snoqualmie Forest/Park Service Information Office, (360) 856-5700.

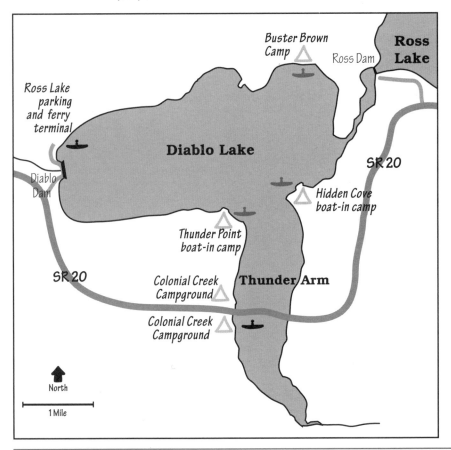

Rating: Beginner to expert

I'll admit right off that this is a favorite of mine. The Colonial Creek National Park campground is quiet and private. You can put your boat in the water at camp and leave it there to jump in when the kayak spirits call, without loading on and off your vehicle every time you want to hit the water.

But, if it is still too civilized for your taste, you can paddle to one of three boat-in only campsites, approximately 2 miles from Colonial Creek. This paddling works for everyone. Our children paddled in Thunder Arm around camp in protected water independently and then, as a group, we headed out the arm into the more exposed Diablo Lake.

On Diablo Lake, the views of the North Cascade peaks are fantastic, and it is not a difficult paddle to get all the way up the cavernous glacial and dam-created lake to Ross Dam. Along the way, you can see Horsetail Falls, only about four miles from Colonial Creek.

The paddle-in sites are small, but pretty. The only problem is that the landings are slightly difficult. You'll need to do a dock landing and the docks float quite high on the water. When water levels are down, beach landings are possible near the campgrounds. Free permits are available at ranger stations and required at boat-in camp- grounds. My favorite spot was Buster Brown Camp because of the view of snowcapped mountains from the site. There was no one around and the campground was tucked in well enough to offer protection from the whistling afternoon winds that come up daily between the dams.

The view from the middle of the lake is awesome, with the looming 9,000 foot North Cascade glaciers all around. The snowy peaks, on a hot sunny day on the water, seem incongruous until you feel the glacial water temperature. The kids swam in the shallows, but the water temperature was too toe-numbing for me.

As for wildlife, they warn of cougar and bear. We were treated to a visit by a golden-eye and her ducklings, many geese with goslings, and a loon. We probably would have seen more, had we not been in a large group, with puppies and children.

Other attractions: Don't miss the superb fudge in every flavor made fresh every Wednesday at the Skagit General Store, 10 miles west in Newhalem. Dam tours and ferry boat rides on the lake between Diablo and Ross dams can be arranged.

Hiking is spectacular, but you are in the North Cascade National Park, where dogs are unwelcome on all trails outside of campgrounds. The Ross Deluxe Meal Tour of Ross Dam boasts a trip 560 feet up the side of Sourdough Mountain on an antique incline railway, a theater presentation on the history of the Skagit, a cruise on Diablo Lake, a tour of the Ross generators through the hydroelectric plant, plus an all-you-can-eat dinner.

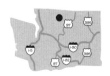

Ross Lake

Maps and charts: Green Trails topographic series, Diablo Dam, WA #48, Washington state map, North Cascades National Park map, Green Trails topographic series, Ross Lake, WA #16.

Access: There are three possible access points to Ross Lake: One option is to put in at the ramp at Diablo Dam, paddle to Ross Dam and call the Ross Lake Resort from the telephone on the side of the powerhouse for a truck to pick you up and portage you over Ross Dam to Ross Lake. Fee, of course.

You can also hike or ferry into the lake and rent boats at the Ross Lake Resort.

A third choice is to put in at the boat ramp at Colonial Creek Campground (see Diablo Lake section), paddle to Ross Dam and call for the portage over Ross Dam.

Mileage: 150 miles from Seattle. Lake mileage: 24 miles long.

Motors: 10 hp motors maximum available for rent on the lake. Jet skis are not allowed anywhere in the North Cascades National Park or the Ross Lake National Recreation Area.

Directions: Take SR 20 east. Turn left at Diablo Dam, then turn off at milepost 127. Drive over the dam to the parking area for Ross Lake Resort. Put in and paddle 4 1/2 miles up Diablo Lake, or hike or ferry in along the same route.

Alternate Route: If you aren't bringing your own boats, take SR 20 east to milepost 134 and hike two miles in to Ross Lake from there.

Alternate Route: Take SR 20 east to Colonial Creek Campground and put in there. Paddle up Diablo Lake and call Ross Lake Resort for portage at the Ross Dam powerhouse telephone.

More information: North Cascades National Park Ranger Station (camping permits), (360) 873-4500, Ext. 39.
Northwest Forest Pass information (needed for parking at Diablo Dam lot and some others), (800) 270-7504.
Ross Lake Resort, (206)386-4437.

Rating: Intermediate to expert

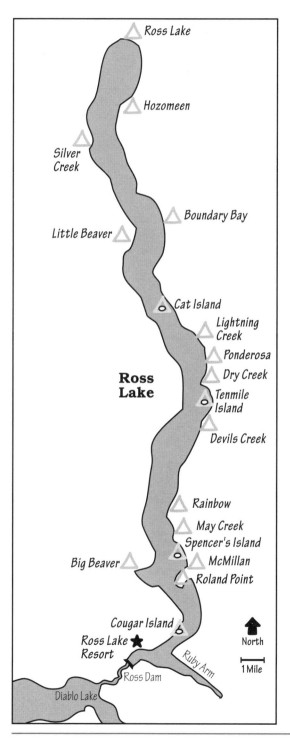

Ross Lake

Hozomeen

Silver Creek

Little Beaver

Boundary Bay

Cat Island

Lightning Creek

Ponderosa

Dry Creek

Ross Lake

Tenmile Island

Devils Creek

Rainbow

May Creek

Spencer's Island

Big Beaver

McMillan

Roland Point

Cougar Island

Ross Lake Resort

Ross Dam

Ruby Arm

Diablo Lake

North

1 Mile

Plan to spend at least one night, if venturing into Ross Lake. The lake takes some planning and expense to get to, but the pay-off is a remote experience well worth the effort.

The lake is dotted with boat-in or hike-in campgrounds. My favorite campground is at Ten-Mile Island, with its view of magnificent waterfalls on the west shore of the lake. Island camping always appeals to me, anyway.

Once, we took the simpler route of paddling in and staying at the Ross Lake Resort. The resort has beau-tiful floating cabins with great views of the peaks jutting up on the south end of the lake. Cabins range from rustic to fully equipped, but all have kitchens and bedding — just bring your own food and clothing.

You'll need a Northwest Forest Pass at certain parking lots, and a backcountry camping permit (free) if you plan to camp on Ross Lake. These are available at the vis-itor information center in Newhalem or at any area ranger station.

The easiest put-in, if you're paddling and portaging, is at the Colonial Creek Campground. Plus, you get to paddle both Diablo Lake and Thunder Arm.

Ross Lake

Signs everywhere warn of bear and cougar. Some campgrounds have bear-proof boxes for stowing gear and food, making camping in bear country easier.

We saw osprey and a loon on the lake, and watched several fishermen hauling in 15-inch native trout.

I rate this lake intermediate to expert because getting in or out with a headwind can be troublesome, and there is no alternative paddle destination once you're committed. Also, steep and rocky side walls mean landing points are minimal, except in designated campgrounds. Even the floating docks at some campgrounds are high and landings can be tricky.

Other attractions: En route on SR 20 is the Sauk Pottery Store, worth the stop if you like hand-thrown pottery. If you're a chocolate lover, stop at The Skagit General Store in Newhalem, where you'll find fresh baked fudge in every flavor — a nice treat at the end of your trip.

Cabins at Ross Lake Resort.

Ross Lake Dam and North Cascades Glaciers from Ross Lake Resort.

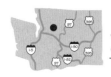

Lake Wenatchee

Maps and charts: US Forest Service Wenatchee National Forest map, USGS topographic map, Wenatchee Lake #145.

Access: Launch possible, for a fee, at the state park at the south end of the lake and Glacier View Campground on the northwest shore.

Mileage: Approximately 100 miles east of Seattle. Lake mileage: Approximately 5.5 miles long and 1 mile across.

Motors: 10 mph speed limit within 100 yards of the beaches.

Directions: Take US 2 toward Leavenworth. Go left on SR 207 and north to Lake Wenatchee.

More information: Reservations Northwest, for state park campground reservations, (800) 452-5687. Nason Creek, Dirty Face and Glacier View campgrounds are first come, first served.
Lake Wenatchee Ranger District, (509) 763-3103.
Leavenworth Outfitters (kayak and canoe rentals), (509) 763-3733.
Leavenworth Summer Theatre, (509) 548-2000.
Leavenworth Visitor Information Center and Chamber of Commerce, (509) 548-5807.

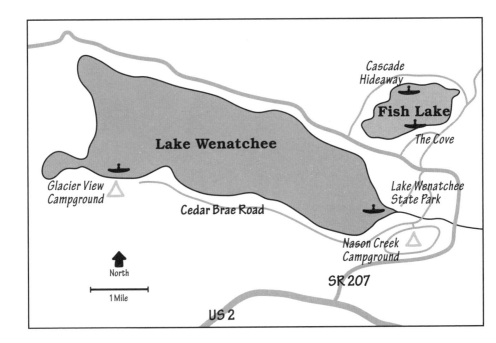

Rating: Intermediate to expert

I s it always windy here? That's the question most commonly posted on the comments board at the lake. The answer is: Usually.

Nonetheless, being a relatively large lake only 100 miles from Seattle, Lake Wenatchee is an easily accessible alpine paddling destination. The snowy peaks are beautiful, the campgrounds, both US Forest Service and state park, are well-maintained, and it is possible to stear clear of motorboats by staying close to shore where it is relatively shallow.

However, jet skis and motorboats abound up and down the middle of the lake and the area is crowded during summer weekends.

For wind protection, try paddling the northwest end of the lake near Squaw Lake, launching at the Glacier View Campground. Glacier View is also a good bet for camping, as you can get waterfront property and launch from camp there.

But for swimming, the east end of the lake is shallowest, and therefore warmest in midsummer.

Unfortunately, most of the lake water remains below 50 degrees year round — not the best place to practice wet exits and re-entries without wetsuits.

Because the lake is windy, cold, and over 200 feet deep, take the same precautions you'd take on the ocean.

As far as wildlife, there are eagle, osprey, deer, and bear roaming. For more extensive birding and fewer jet skiers, you may want to head 2 more miles up the road to Fish Lake.

Other attractions: The town of Leavenworth, known as little Bavaria, is only 20 miles to the east. It is a cute tourist town with all the amenities you could ask for. Among the annual events in Leavenworth are the Wenatchee River Salmon Festival, Quilt Show, and Oktoberfest, to name just a few. Also, the Leavenworth Summer Theater presents musicals under the stars. Incidentally, Leavenworth is much closer to Lake Wenatchee than the town of Wenatchee is.

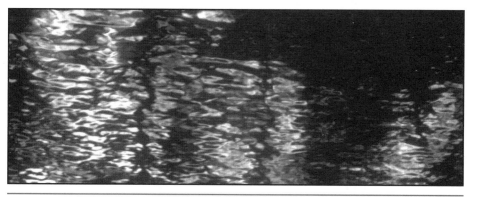

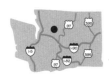

Fish Lake

Maps and charts: US Forest Service Wenatchee National Forest map, Washington state map.

Access: Launch from either of two private campgrounds – Cascade Hideaway on Forest Service Road #6402 and the Cove Resort on Forest Service Road #6401. Fees collected at both.

Mileage: Approximately 100 miles east of Seattle. Lake mileage: 2 miles long, 1 mile wide.

Motors: The small lake size keeps speed boats and jet skis away. Trolling motors aplenty.

Directions: Take US 2 toward Leavenworth, then north on SR 207, following signs to Fish Lake.

More information: Cascade Hideaway cabins, (509) 763-5104.
The Cover Resort, camping and canoe rentals, (509) 763-3130.
Lake Wenatchee Ranger District, (509) 763-3103.

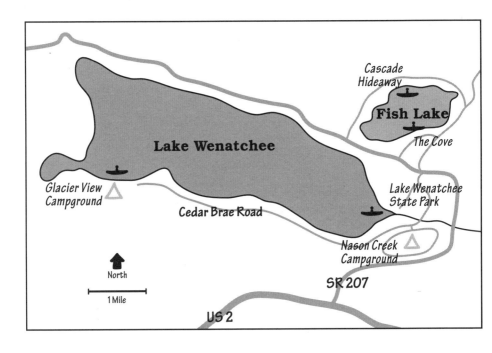

Rating: Beginner

In the same pristine area as Lake Wenatchee, this lake is quieter, smaller and generally has a more remote feel than Lake Wenatchee.

Just ask the birds. This is a preferred spot for many bird species, including several duck species, killdeer, several types of swallow, hawk, owl, (including the great horned), hairy and pileated woodpecker, calliope and rufous hummingbird, black-capped and mountain chickadee, black-headed and evening grosbeak, sharp-shinned and red-tailed hawk, yellow and yellow-rumped warbler, eagle, and osprey.

As for the paddling, the lake is small. There is a 150-acre marshy area at the west end, which can be viewed by boat only. The floating bog is sensitive and should not be trodden upon.

If you enjoy fishing from a kayak or canoe, this is a good place for it. Brown trout, rainbow trout, and yellow perch are in the lake.

The Cove Resort rents canoes, if you need one. The Cascade Hideaway has a launch also and welcomes paddlers to put in there for a fee, even if they aren't staying at their resort.

The lake is frozen over in winter, so if you plan to paddle, wait until the spring thaw.

Other attractions: There are plenty of hiking trails and mountain biking opportunities nearby. Also, the towns of Leavenworth and Cashmere are near, to the southeast. In Cashmere, Chelan County Historical Museum is large, and houses Native American artifacts and natural history and pioneer exhibits, including a pioneer village. River rafting on the Wenatchee River is also popular.

Lake Chelan

Maps and charts: Oregon and Washington state maps, US Forest Service Wenatchee National Forest map.

Access: Ramps at Lake Chelan State Park, Twenty Five Mile Creek State Park, and several sites in the town of Chelan.

Mileage: 300 + miles from Portland, 190 miles from Seattle. Lake mileage: 55 miles long and 2 miles across.

Motors: Motors restricted only near shore and around non-motorized vessels.

Directions: From Portland, go out I-84 east and take US 97 north.

From Seattle, take US 2 outside of Everett to US 97 heading north.

More information: Washington State Park camping reservations, (800) 452-5687.
State Park information, (800) 233-0321.
Chelan Chamber of Commerce, 800-4CHELAN.
Charter Passenger Freight Services information, (509) 682-2224.
Barge service (for boat transport), (509) 682-4584.
Pedal Paddle Lake Chelan, (509) 682-9211.
Stehekin Lodge, (509) 682-4494.
Stehekin Log Cabins, (509) 682-7742.

Rating: Beginner to expert

L ake Chelan's appeal for paddlers is the dry heat. Many Northwest runaways thrive in it. Aside from that, the south end of the lake is a motor mecca making it less appealing for paddlers. Jet skiers are everywhere, including many beginners, as there are jet ski rentals all over the town of Chelan. Paddle near shore and be especially watchful on the south third of the lake.

If you are willing to camp, you can paddle away from most of the noise by heading to the north end of Lake Chelan. A two to three day trip takes you to the small community of Stehekin.

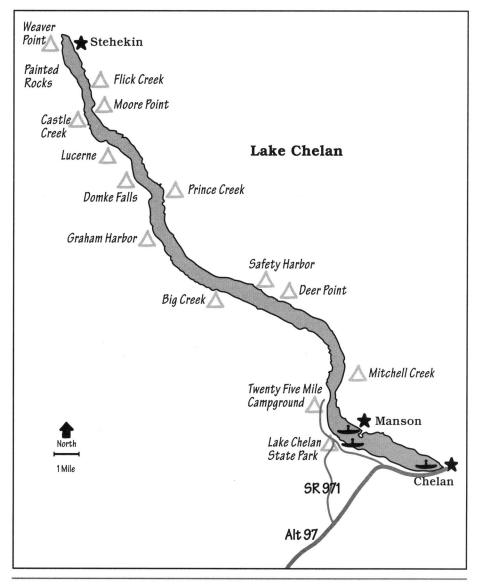

Lake Chelan

If you venture up the lake, you'll be treated to unbelievable scenery along the lake's gorge, scoured by glaciers some 1,700 years ago.

Though campgrounds freckle both sides of the lake, there is limited camping available at Flick Creek and only one campsite available at Domke Falls. Between Safety Harbor and Price Creek, on the east side of the lake, is shear cliff. Paddle the west side if you think you might need to make rest stops. Great waterfalls await your oggling, but the most unique attraction to this long paddle north is the hieroglyphics seen at Painted Rocks.

Once you've reached Stehekin, you can paddle or barge back down the lake. You need to prearrange your boat transportation if you aren't paddling both ways.

Kayak or canoe rentals are available in a few places but the man in the know about paddling Lake Chelan is John Page Jr., owner of Pedal Paddle Lake Chelan, where you can rent kayaks, take a lesson, or book a guided tour.

As for wildlife, aside from the jet skiers, you could see bear and cougar. Plenty of eagle, osprey and other bird life, too.

Other attractions: In the dusty old west climate, I think of rodeos. Sure enough, the Chelan Rodeo comes every year in late July. The town of Chelan also has a farmer's market, children's park, including bumper boats and mini golf, and extensive tourist services at Campbell Resort, lakeside in Chelan. In Stehekin, the full-service restaurant and lodge are a welcome sight to hikers and boaters when they finally reach the north end of the lake.

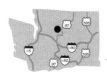

Entiat Lake

Maps and charts: US Forest Service Lake Wenatchee National Forest map, Washington state map.

Access: Lake Entiat Park boat ramp, between Wenatchee and Chelan, on the west side of the Columbia River, along US 97A.

Mileage: 290 miles from Portland, 200 miles from Seattle.

Motors: No restrictions, but many fewer boaters than south Chelan.

Directions: Follow directions to Chelan, stopping on 97A before the town of Entiat, north of the Rocky Reach Dam.

More information: Entiat Ranger District, (509) 784-1511.
Entiat Valley Chamber of Commerce, (800) 353-9500.
Entiat City Park camping reservations, (800) 7Entiat.
Rocky Reach Dam, (509) 663-7522.

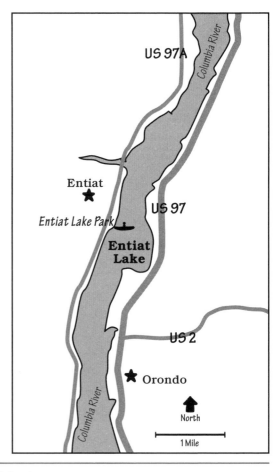

Rating: Intermediate to expert

If the arid environment of Central Washington appeals to you, but the heavy motorboat use does not, try paddling north of the Rocky Reach Dam, on a long slow stretch of the Columbia River.

Entiat Park is very nicely maintained and has a boat ramp for easy launching. The lake gets windy, as do all the tunnel-like, dam-formed lakes, and it is because of the wind that this trip earned an intermediate-to-expert rating. But, when the air is still, beginners can enjoy this area, too. The best paddling times are early morning and sunset.

With highway on both sides, this isn't the most wilderness paddling ever, but it is a nice spot to be on the water, when it's still raining in western Oregon and Washington.

Expect to see a bald eagle or two. They are prevalent in the area.

Other attractions: If you are going to take advantage of the dammed lakes, you might as well view the construction feat of a dam. Rocky Reach does it right with their tours and grounds. Grand Coulee Dam isn't far off and is known for the late night laser shows in summer. Wenatchee is 7 miles to the south and has an annual apple blossom festival, among other events in summer. Mountain biking is also big in the area.

Appendix

Kayak & Canoe Clubs:

Cascade Canoe Club of Salem
Jim Bradley
Oregon Canoe Sports
2366 State Street #B
Salem, OR 97301

Green Lakes Small Craft Center, home of
Seattle Canoe and Kayak Club
5900 W. Greenlake Way N.
Seattle, WA 98103
(206) 684-4074

Lesbian and Gay Sea Kayakers
1122 E. Pike #896
Seattle, WA 98122-3934

Mountaineers
300 3rd Ave. West
Seattle, WA 98119

North Sound Sea Kayak Association
PO Box 1520
Everett, WA 98201

Olympic Kayak Club
22293 Clear Creek Road NW
Poulsbo, WA 98370

Oregon Ocean Paddling Society (OOPS)
PO Box 69641
Portland, OR 97201

Paddletrails Canoe Club
PO Box 24932 Seattle, WA 98124
(206) 444-4313

Port Orchard Paddle Club
2398 Jefferson Ave. SE
Port Orchard, WA 98366

Puget Sound Paddle Club
PO Box 111892
Tacoma, WA 98411-1892

Seattle Sea Kayak Club
13906 123 Avenue NE.
Kirkland, WA 98034

Southern Oregon Paddlers
PO Box 2111
Bandon, OR 97411

Tacoma Outdoor Pursuits
Tacoma, WA
(253) 474-8155

Washington Kayak Club
PO Box 24264
Seattle, WA 98124

Washington Water Trails Association
4649 Sunnyside Ave. North, Suite #305
Seattle, WA 98103
(206) 545-9161

Yakima Kayak Club
PO Box 11147
Yakima, WA 98909

Whatcom Association of Kayak
Enthusiasts (WAKE)
Dave Wallin
PO Box 1952
Bellingham, WA 98227
(360) 671-6883

Appendix

Retail Sales and Rentals:

Alder Creek Kayak and Canoe:
Portland
250 NE Tomahawk Island Drive
Portland, OR 97217
(503) 285-0464

Bend
345 SW Century Drive
Bend, OR 97702
(541) 389-0890

Bend Outdoor
Bend, OR
(541) 389-7191

Ebb and Flow Paddlesports
604 SW Nebraska Avenue
Portland, OR 97201
(503) 245-1756

Moss Bay Kayaks
(southeast side of Lake Union, by TGIF)
Seattle, WA
(206) 682-2031

Nehalem Bay Kayak Company
395 Highway 101
Wheeler, OR
(877)-KAYAKCO or (503) 368-6055

Northern Lights
PO Box 4289 Bellingham, WA 98227
(800) 754-7402

Northwest Outdoor Center
2100 Westlake Avenue N., Suite #1
Seattle, WA 98109
(206) 281-9694

Pacific Wave
Warrenton, OR
(503) 861-0866

Portland River Company
315 SW Montgomery, Suite #330
Portland, OR 97201
(503)229-0551

Powder House
Bend, OR
(541) 389-6234

REI:
Eugene
3rd and Washington
Eugene, OR 97401
(541) 465-1800

Bellingham
400 36th Street
Bellingham, WA 98225
(360) 647-8955

Federal Way
2565 S. Gateway Center Place
Federal Way, WA 98003
(253) 941-4994

Kennewick
129 N. Ely Street
Kennewick, WA 99336
(509) 734-8989

Lynnwood
4200 194th Street SW
Lynnwood, WA 98036
(425) 774-1300

Portland
1798 Jantzen Beach Center
Portland, OR 97217
(503) 283-1300

Redmond
7500 166th Avenue NE
Redmond, OR 98052
(425) 882-1158

Appendix

Rentals and Tours:

REI cont.:
Seattle
222 Yale Avenue North
Seattle, WA 98109
(206) 223-1944
(888) 873-1938

Spokane
North 1125 Monroe Street
Spokane, WA 99201
(509) 328-9900

Tualitin
7410 SW Bridgeport Road
Tigard, OR 97224
(503) 624-8600

Skookum Bay Outfitters
Aberdeen, WA
(360) 533-0825

Whalecraft Folding Kayaks
4011 Fremont Avenue North
Seattle WA 98103
(206) 634-0628

Adventurous Spirit Kayaking
Whidbey Island
(360) 321-5453

Agua Verde (rentals and food on the north end of Lake Union)
Seattle, WA
(595) 455-8570

Deception Pass Adventure Center
(877) 568-6877

Nehalem River Inn
Mohler, OR
(800) 368-6499

Nehalem Bay Kayak Company
Wheeler, OR
(503) 368-6055

Northwest Discoveries of Tigard leads tours for many local parks districts.
(503) 624-4829

Pedal Paddle Lake Chelan
Chelan, WA
(509) 682-9211

Skamokawa Kayak and Canoe Center and B & B
1391 W. State Route 4
Skamokawa, WA 98647
(888) 920-2777

Wheeler on the Bay Lodge and Marina
(800) 469-3204

Index

Maps are indicated with **bold** print.
Photographs are indicated with *italic* print.